© 2009 by Pearson Education, Inc.
Publishing as FT Press
Upper Saddle River, New Jersey 07458

FT Press offers excellent discounts on
this book when ordered in quantity
for bulk purchases or special sales.
For more information, please contact
U.S. Corporate and Government
Sales, 1-800-382-3419, corpsales@
pearsontechgroup.com. For sales outside
the U.S., please contact International
Sales at international@pearson.com.

Printed in the United States of America

First Printing January 2009

ISBN-10: 0-13-702207-7
ISBN-13: 978-0-13-702207-6

Pearson Education LTD.
Pearson Education Australia PTY,
Limited.
Pearson Education Singapore, Pte. Ltd.
Pearson Education North Asia, Ltd.
Pearson Education Canada, Ltd.
Pearson Educación de Mexico, S.A. de C.V.
Pearson Education—Japan
Pearson Education Malaysia, Pte. Ltd.

Library of Congress Cataloging-in-Publication Data on file

Vice President, Publisher
Tim Moore

**Associate Publisher and
Director of Marketing**
Amy Neidlinger

Editorial Assistant
Pamela Boland

Operations Manager
Gina Kanouse

Digital Marketing Manager
Julie Phifer

Publicity Manager
Laura Czaja

Assistant Marketing Manager
Megan Colvin

Cover Designer
Mark van Bronkhorst,
TypoBrand

Design Manager
Sandra Schroeder

Managing Editor
Kristy Hart

Senior Project Editor
Lori Lyons

Proofreader
San Dee Phillips

Indexer
Erika Millen

Compositor
Nonie Ratcliff

Manufacturing Buyer
Dan Uhrig

BARACK, INC.

WINNING BUSINESS LESSONS
OF THE OBAMA CAMPAIGN

**BARRY LIBERT
AND RICK FAULK**

BARACK, INC.

CONTENTS

ACKNOWLEDGMENTS

We, like most authors, have many people to thank. Our appreciation goes to the 225 employees at Mzinga, among them Dan Bruns, Drew Darnborough, Susan Koutalakis, Josh Melvin, Mike Migliorinio, Patrick Moran, Gina Odryna, Eve Sangenito, Alexa Scordato, Nancy Sheen, Jim Storer, Joe Tremonte, and Sabrina Walker, who are helping us build the best social software business on the planet. Our thanks, also, to the first-rate team at Pearson: Tim Moore, Amy Neidlinger, Gina Kanouse, Megan Colvin, Sandra Schroeder, Lori Lyons, Erika Millen, Nonie Ratcliff, and San Dee Phillips.

Our heartfelt appreciation also goes to Donna Sammons Carpenter, Maurice Coyle, and the other talented writers, researchers, and editors at Wordworks, Inc.: Ruth Hlavacek, Larry Martz, Molly Sammons Morris, Cindy Butler Sammons, Robert Shnayerson, and Robert W. Stock. Finally, we are indebted to our literary agent Helen Rees, who never flagged in her support of Barack Obama and this project.

AUTHORS

Barry Libert is chairman and **Rick Faulk** CEO of Mzinga, a leading provider of social software solutions that help major corporations around the world create online communities for marketing, customer support, and learning. It manages more than 14,000 communities and has over 60 million unique visitors every month.

Libert is a pioneer in using communities and Web 2.0 technologies to help enterprises thrive and accelerate business growth. He was co-author of the recently published *We Are Smarter than Me*, a critically acclaimed book created in collaboration with Wharton School Publishing that used the Wiki-based contributions of more than 4,000 people to illustrate how businesses could profit from the wisdom of crowds. A one-time McKinsey and Company consultant, Libert has also co-authored two other highly regarded books about the business value of information and relationships.

Faulk has spent his career working in the field
of marketing, on-demand collaboration, and
software-as-a-service technologies. He has 21 years
of executive experience at high-tech companies,
among them WebEx, Intranets.com, PictureTel,
Shiva Corporation, and Lotus. Early in his career, he
also founded First Software, which grew to sales of
more than $175 million in less than four years and
was ranked on one of *Inc.* magazine's lists of fastest-
growing companies in the United States.

To the three people that really matter in my life:
One, my wife Ellen,
two, my son Adam, and,
three, my son Michael.
—Barry Libert

To my wife Kathy and
my two children,
Brian and Ashley, who make
everything worthwhile.
—Rick Faulk

WHO AMONG US EVER FULLY BELIEVED THAT A CINDERELLA CANDIDATE COULD SOAR OUT OF ILLINOIS OBSCURITY AND BECOME THE 44TH PRESIDENT OF THE UNITED STATES, CONFOUNDING DOZENS OF WORLD-RENOWNED POLITICOS IN THE PROCESS? YET BARACK OBAMA MANAGED TO BEAT THE REPUBLICAN PARTY AT ITS OWN GAME WITH DISCIPLINE, ORGANIZATION, AND MASSIVE FUNDRAISING.

INTRODUCTION

From his cooler-than-cool leadership style to his use of Internet-based social technologies to his basic message of change, Barack Obama showed businesspeople that they have a lot to learn from a savvy politician.

In the flush of Obama's triumph, we need to recall his initial hurdles, all seemingly insurmountable. Here was a truly exotic presidential hopeful—a stranger with a Muslim-sounding name, an African father, a white American mother, a Hawaiian childhood, a Harvard law degree, and a political resume of perhaps 25 words or less. As he put it in his victory speech, "I was never the likeliest candidate for office."

All sorts of moves, from tried-and-true tactics to cutting-edge strategies, turned Obama's candidacy from improbable to inevitable. He assembled a first-class team of staffers who ran a nearly flawless campaign; he attracted tens of thousands of volunteers, many of them so dedicated that they left their jobs or dropped out of school to work on his election; and he collected an unprecedented amount of money, both from small contributors and big traditional donors. But we were especially riveted by the campaign's prodigious use of social networking. That's a subject we have studied in depth, and Barack Obama is tuned to our wavelength. He turned a 50-state presidential campaign into one enormous online community. His networking inspired millions of people across the United States to join a national crusade, pooling their skills, time, and dollars to achieve a decisive victory. As a result, American (and perhaps world) politics will never be the same.

We believe Obama's political pioneering set a brilliant standard for any business seeking to prosper in the Web 2.0 world of the 21st century. Hence this book: Obama's campaign saga annotated for business use.

We combined our own observations with those of a diverse group of media whose expertise was on display during this long, dramatic campaign. We interviewed Obama supporters, collected an array of superb reports from a variety of sources, and paid close heed to the blogosphere's unprecedented election coverage—the latter a concatenation of diverse views and voices ranging from Politico to Twitter that did much to make 2008 a turning point in politics. Our goal was to tease out the relevance of this historic campaign to business leaders everywhere.

Let's get started.

GETTING DOWN TO
BUSINESS MAY BE
PASSÉ.

GETTING UP TO
POLITICS COULD BE
THE WAVE OF OUR
FUTURE.

CHAPTER 1
SUCCESS YOU CAN BELIEVE
IN—AND EMULATE

Remember "dollar-a-year men"? They were Corporate America's best and brightest, the take-charge CEOs who volunteered to save the U.S. government from itself during grave crises, including both world wars. Back then, everyone assumed Washington politicians lacked the brains and gumption to solve national emergencies. To their rescue rode business geniuses like Robert McNamara, the Ford Motor Company "Whiz Kid" who ran the Pentagon during the Vietnam War. Because the government can't accept free services, these men charged a symbolic dollar per year, making them even more selfless and presumably competent.

Soon it became received wisdom that the business bench is crowded with star players able and eager to clean up the mess in Washington. As a result, politicians began donning business masks. Cheers erupted when politicians claimed managerial experience and gravely pledged to run the American government "like a business." Indeed, various business leaders (Ross Perot, the two Romneys, Mitt and his father George) took the idea further and ran for president themselves.

So how does the notion of business *uber* politics fare today? What if it turns out that business has more to learn from politics than the other way around? What

if Barack Obama's extraordinary campaign was a feat
of managing ideas, people, and technology on a scale
so massive and demanding that historians rank it as
a sort of Manhattan Project of presidential politics?

Our book offers valuable reasons for business leaders
not to wait for historians. We invite—urge—you
to examine Obama's campaign performance right
now. Pore over its peak moments. Find all sorts of
possible trails to business turnarounds—we did. If
you do, too, e-mail the dean of your favorite business
school, urging a crash course in Obama campaigning
and leadership, annotated for future CEOs. As the
opening of this chapter suggests, getting down to
business may be passé. Getting up to politics could
be the wave of our future.

BUSINESS BY THE PEOPLE AND FOR THE PEOPLE.

Many of the lessons ahead are brand-new and
previously untried ideas so innovative that cautious
souls might hesitate to use them. Others are familiar,
road-tested tactics so commonplace that politicians
and businesspeople alike may be tempted to ignore
them. Taken together, they created the Obama
campaign—a unique set of moves that we can all
learn to adapt. Let's start counting the ways.

1. *He stayed cool.* Barack Obama was unflappable in the debates and showed no anger at underhanded attacks. Even more unlikely, he was able to ignore all distractions and remain firmly on message for a marathon race lasting nearly two years. With his relative inexperience, Obama focused unrelentingly on the nation's need for change.

How can a business leader cultivate Obama's cool? Among the specific lessons shared in Chapter 2, "Be Cool," he learned to keep his focus on the main goal, ignoring all distractions. He knew how to correct problems without blaming people for them. He could play hardball when that was necessary, and he could blow off his emotions without affecting his campaign. He knew how to adjust to the needs of the moment. Perhaps best of all, he learned from Abraham Lincoln's example to lead without losing his humility.

So, too, must business leaders react calmly to hard times and unforeseen emergencies. That means that they must build sound organizations, plan for contingencies, and be ready to implement their plans, while sticking as close as they can to Obama's character traits. Just as Obama won over voters by seeming presidential, business leaders can win over their people, their suppliers, and their customers by remaining cool, rational, and statesmanlike—all the while moving smartly to beat their competitors.

2. *He unleashed social technologies.* Obama won the 2008 election by seven percentage points, in large part because he used all the social technologies of our time—blogs, discussion boards, viral videos, texting, and cell-phone networks—to connect with his constituencies. He created a grassroots community (My. BarackObama.com) to market his campaign and raise an unprecedented flood of capital.

Among the points to emulate in Chapter 3, "Be Social," Obama learned to cultivate the new grassroots constituency that the Internet has made accessible. With copious lists of voter registrations, swing voters, and possible donors, he built a seamless community of supporters, volunteers, and converts to the cause. He made himself bulletproof against the cheap political shots that he himself refused to use against his opponents. He used customer-relations software to create true customer relationships within his community. And he used text messaging and cell-phone networks to expand and reinforce his community.

Companies do themselves an extreme disservice if they forgo the benefits of all these social technologies—for instance, more customers, lower costs, additional leads, higher efficiency, and greater profits.

3. *He embraced and embodied change.* Business leaders must enable change, not defend the status quo. By no coincidence, Obama's preemption of "change" neatly undercut his two main opponents, Hillary Clinton and John McCain, both veteran Washington hands. Not realizing they were working against themselves, they ran mainly on their past "experience" and readiness to govern—a message badly out of sync with America's weariness with Washington and hunger for new faces and new ideas.

For Obama, however, "change" meant more than a political slogan. To win, he knew he would have to develop a clear vision of the future and share it with the voters. Among the business insights: That vision would have to confront the realities facing the nation and put them in context. He knew that when he held the high ground, it would be foolish to back off, and that he needed a strong team with a minimum of squabbling and infighting. He knew the power of the personal touch and the necessity of getting information straight and unfiltered. And above all, he had the ability to assess himself clearly and objectively—a crucial talent for any leader, business or political.

If our leaders aren't willing to embrace change and new ideas, our economy will never recover from the current meltdown in the financial markets. We need to recognize that financial systems and markets are flawed and must be corrected. The same is true for businesses and their leaders. If they have not yet answered or even recognized the need for drastic action, they need to make way for others. But to make change work for the good, they must learn the lessons Obama's campaign can teach.

Perhaps Barack Obama's most important lesson is his basic unspoken premise, a principle that traces to his long-time role model, Abraham Lincoln: Government must be by the people and for the people. It's a principle that translates into a winning motto for us: business by the people and for the people.

Our country is now entangled in a major recession. But in our history, setbacks invariably generate rebirth. More than likely, the hardships ahead will trigger what we need, a potentially massive change in mind-set. Ordinary people and government officials alike will learn the merits of *Poor Richard's Almanac* and the hazards of too much debt. And businesses will finally zero in on what matters most to them—profits, products and services, people, and the communities they form.

As Barack Obama kept saying during his primary campaign, the time for change is now: "We are the ones we've been waiting for. We are the change that we seek." That was a remarkable statement for any American politician. By conventional standards, it was far too mystical to appeal to the pragmatic, down-to-earth swing voters who decide elections. Yet, somehow it resonated.

Of course, Obama's "we" boils down to individual change and responsibility. In the end, it is up to us—the heads of our businesses, the leaders of our communities. It's we who must keep our cool, invest in social technologies, and accept the reality of change.

IT'S WE WHO MUST KEEP OUR COOL, INVEST IN SOCIAL TECHNOLOGIES, AND ACCEPT THE REALITY OF CHANGE.

The whole purpose of this book is to help light the way with ready-to-work lessons learned from Obama's remarkable campaign. In the words of Mohandas Gandhi, "You must be the change you wish to see in the world." As the rest of this book argues, believe in change, act on it, and then we will truly have businesses by the people and for the people.

Yes, we can.

THE INDISPENSABLE
QUALITY OF A LEADER
WHOSE DECISIONS
AND ACTIONS CAN
CHANGE PEOPLE'S
LIVES IS HIS COOL—HIS
CALM RATIONALITY,
STEADINESS UNDER
PRESSURE, AND ABILITY
TO STAY ON MESSAGE
AND CONTROL STRONG
EMOTIONS.

CHAPTER 2
BE COOL

Barack Obama, as a memorable YouTube video portrayed him, is the Mr. Spock of politicians— unflappable, unemotional, cool to the point of seeming Vulcan. Obama's speechwriter, Jon Favreau, has said his reaction to winning the Iowa caucuses was hardly different from his response to losing the New Hampshire primary, when he turned to an aide and remarked calmly, "This will turn out to have been a good thing."

This aloofness can tend to turn off voters who crave more accessible public figures. But over the course of the long campaign, his imperturbable, confident strength under fire may have been his key asset. Brushing aside the many distractions and personal attacks, he stayed on message for months at a time. He looked, in a word, presidential, and in the end the voters valued that far more than any guy-next-door affability and easy charm.

That's a lesson for business leaders everywhere. When you're at the helm of a big operation, it never hurts to be friendly, informal and accessible; a touch of human warmth wins hearts and trust. But, as we note in the opening of this chapter, the indispensable quality of a leader whose decisions and actions can change people's lives is his cool—his calm rationality, steadiness under pressure, and ability to stay on message and control strong emotions.

A leader who shows anger usually seems petty and faintly ridiculous. For all his business smarts and leadership talent, the impulsive Ted Turner was vulnerable to emotional manipulation and found himself outmaneuvered and sidelined in his merger with Time Warner. And when any leader panics, it's a signal to his or her people that the situation is even worse than they thought.

Temperament is determined largely by genetics, and some are more naturally prone than others to being swayed by emotions. But psychologists say that people can teach themselves to react calmly to emotional situations rather than fly off the handle. George Washington, revered as a calm and composed leader, was just the reverse as a young man, fiery and impulsive. "He cultivated his cool through sheer willpower," says Dean Keith Simonton, a professor of psychology at the University of California at Davis. As a young man taking over his grandfather's decaying business empire, Henry Ford II had to muster the coolness to confront and banish Harry Bennett, the thuggish chief of security whose goons all but ruled Ford's main plant. In fact, nearly every successful business leader has a tale to tell of emotions mastered and fears stowed away.

Barack Obama learned early that a mask of calm was as good as body armor. In his memoir *Dreams from*

My Father, he tells of disarming his mother when she came to his room to upbraid him about his lazy performance in school and his general fecklessness. Rather than argue or yell, he gave her "a reassuring smile and patted her hand and told her not to worry." She backed off, and so, he found, did most people as long as he was "courteous and smiled and made no sudden moves... . They were relieved—such a pleasant surprise to find a well-mannered young black man who didn't seem angry all the time."

Obama was also good at focusing on what to do about a problem instead of reacting emotionally. His staffers said a turning point in the campaign came for them in a conference call about the crisis overwhelming the financial world. Obama spelled out his plans: He would consult with Treasury Secretary Henry Paulson and Federal Reserve Chairman Ben Bernanke; then he would talk to Senate Majority Leader Harry Reid; then he would decide where he stood on the proposed bailout of the banking system. For the first time, his aides said, they got a feeling of what he would be like if he won the election. "That was the moment," said his communications director, Dan Pfeiffer, when Obama "began looking like a President and not a presidential candidate."

For Obama's strategist David Axelrod, the payoff came when Obama resisted the politically expedient tactic of opposing the bailout. That would have been catnip for voters outraged at seeing their taxes used to rescue greedy bankers, but Obama rejected it as irresponsible, too big a risk to the financial system. Axelrod told a reporter for *The New Yorker* magazine that he had known and trusted Obama for 16 years, "but you never know how someone is gonna handle the vagaries and vicissitudes of a presidential race." The election process can be "barbaric and sometimes ridiculous," he said, but "the thing I love about it is that at the end of the day you can't hide who you are." And Barack Obama stayed true to himself.

To run his campaign, Obama chose people close to his own personality type—as he put it, "people who are calm, who don't get too high and don't get too low." The result was a campaign style that reporters soon dubbed "No drama Obama." But by any measure, the campaign staffers were successful in the job they were chosen to do: They pleased the candidate, functioned smoothly and expertly, and won the race.

The "no-drama" rule was for real. Alyssa Mastromonaco, Obama's director of scheduling, was one of the few campaign aides who had actual experience on the job, having served in John Kerry's presidential race in 2004. She was used to a more free-swinging style, and when she blew up in a conference call, she got a reproving visit from a delegation of fellow staffers. "They were like, 'Alyssa, this is a campaign where you need to respect other people's opinions, and you can't be a bitch,'" she told *The New Yorker.* "I was like, 'Oh my God, these guys are serious!'"

It was the campaign manager, David Plouffe, who maintained the low-key tone. In sharp contrast to most political honchos, Plouffe wasn't a screamer; as strategist Steve Elmendorf put it, "With David, you do your job, get it done, and keep your head down."

THE REAL KEY TO CULTIVATING YOUR COOL IS LEARNING TO ZERO IN ON A PRACTICAL RESPONSE TO A PROBLEM.

Obama was the unquestioned chief, presiding over meetings, cross-examining his staffers, and insisting on getting opinions from everyone at the table. "He assumes if you haven't said anything, you might disagree," said his senior adviser Valerie Jarrett. "I can't tell you the number of times he's looked at me when I haven't said a word, and he looks right in my eyes and says, 'What are you thinking?'" Obama praised good work publicly, thanking local organizers at his rallies just as enthusiastically as he thanked the mayor or the governor of the state, and he gave his staff straight, blunt feedback. "If he's happy, you know it," said Jarrett. "If he prefers to do something different, you know it. He's not shy about being clear. I think there are a lot of CEOs who don't give straight and direct feedback."

She's right about that, and Obama's campaign should be a model for business leaders everywhere.

In other words, whether Barack Obama was born cool or carefully learned it, the cool was for real.

BE COOL: IGNORE THE SIDESHOWS, KEEP YOUR EYE ON THE CENTER RING—THE LESSONS OF SARAH PALIN.

If Barack Obama's palms ever get sweaty, he sure doesn't show it. But his staffers could have used a dusting of powder shortly after John McCain picked Sarah Palin as his running mate. The choice was a pure McCain move—impulsive, a bit quirky, and defiant, with the air of a Hail Mary pass. "We just threw long," said one of his aides, watching McCain introduce her. And at first, the Obama people saw Palin as an outright gift, an unseasoned candidate whose choice undermined McCain's argument that Obama wasn't ready for the Oval Office. "Okay, game over," said one staffer on the next morning's conference call.

Then the doubts began to set in. The Alaska governor was feisty, independent, a bracing breath of the North Country. And she was a natural politician. Watching her gleefully mock Obama in her acceptance speech, *Newsweek* reported that three of Hillary Clinton's people who had signed up with Obama looked at each other glumly. "This woman's trouble," one of them said.

In the next few days, as Palin drew bigger and bigger crowds to McCain's rallies and the campaign press obsessed over her, the Obama staff's nervousness only grew. McCain's poll numbers were rising, in part because Palin was attracting a surge of women to his flag. In the no-drama ethos of Obama's staff, no real panic was evident. But as a senior aide told *Newsweek*, "People went a little Kerry and Dukakis there for a couple of days"—an ominous reference to the sour pessimism of those Democratic campaigns. Chief strategist David Axelrod went around assuring people that the Palin bubble would burst sooner or

later, and campaign manager David Plouffe urged
everyone to calm down.

The Obama team worked to remain unperturbed.
Worsening poll numbers could be attributed to the
typical post-convention bounce for McCain. And,
in any case, Sarah Palin wasn't the main attraction,
just a sideshow—right? People vote for the head of
the ticket, not the veep. What mattered was to keep
focused on the real game. And a senior aide carried
that message through the Chicago headquarters,
ordering the Palin-dazed staffers to "get her out of
your head! It's McCain!"

In Bill Clinton's 1992 campaign, strategist James
Carville had put up a celebrated sign—"It's the
Economy, Stupid"—to keep his staffers' eyes on
the ball. And in similar fashion, business leaders
who prize solid results over protocol and business
precedent are learning new ways of doing business.
Office discipline, office hours, and even offices
themselves are mere sideshows for companies that
have learned to get results using flextime, job-
sharing plans, and telecommuting. And what may
come as a surprise, the U.S. Patent and Trademark
Office is in the forefront of this movement, with
some 40 percent of its employees doing at least some
of their work outside the office. Some individuals
work at home, while others use the agency's telework

offices, which depend on satellite setups in locations anywhere from 16 to 80 miles from downtown Washington. Patent examiners in a telework pilot study showed a productivity gain of 10 percent, with no loss of quality.

The success of the program earned the Patent Office recognition from *BusinessWeek* magazine as one of the best places in America to launch or round out a career. *Families* magazine called the government agency one of the most family-friendly places to work in the Washington area.

When you're focusing steadily on what matters, you don't let anything distract you—not custom, not pride, not even the loss of your carefully managed business persona. It's hardly usual, for example, for a successful and respected physician to allow a nurse or an orderly to confront him in public, demanding cash and getting it. As executive vice president of the prestigious Methodist Hospital in Houston, Texas, Dr. Marc Boom might be expected to command more than a little deference as he walks the hospital's corridors and strolls in and out of patients' rooms. On occasion, however, a hospital employee will pop up in front of him, saying, "Stop and give me 20!" A bit sheepishly, Boom pulls out his wallet and hands over a $20 bill.

The mini-drama is Boom's own idea, part of his crusade to keep his hospital focused on attacking the plague of hospital-acquired infections that has hit medical institutions all over the country. To dramatize the simple solution to the problem— making medical personnel wash their hands between patients—Boom challenged hospital employees to follow him and other executives on their rounds. Any of the brass caught neglecting to wash their hands on their way into or out of a patient's room must forfeit $20 on the spot.

It's a little rough on the dignity, but the results more than offset any discomfort. Methodist Hospital's rate of compliance with the hand-washing rule, which had been way down in the 40 percent range before Boom's initiative, has shot up to more than 90 percent, and infections have dropped significantly.

Keeping its focus on John McCain, not Sarah Palin, paid off for the Obama campaign. The McCain camp's vetting of Palin had been a bit spotty. The Internet buzzed with rumors that Palin wanted to privatize Social Security, that she belonged to a party that favored seceding from the United States and making Alaska its own country, that she read the ultraconservative John Birch Society magazine. But as the campaign played them, these rumors—plus Palin's ousting of Alaska's public safety commissioner, who refused to fire her former brother-in-law—weren't so much damaging Palin as highlighting McCain's shoot-from-the-hip style of decision making. Could we afford such impulsive behavior in the White House? Voters wondered.

When word leaked from the McCain campaign that Palin had been fitted out with a $150,000 wardrobe, McCain's own staffers started sniping at her as an uncontrollable "diva." And with that, Sarah Palin had become a liability for McCain and an asset for Obama.

Barack Obama defeated Palin without ever attacking her. He had kept his cool while keeping the focus on John McCain, the real target, and that was enough.

BE COOL: FIX THE PROBLEM, FORGET THE BLAME—THE LESSONS OF LOSING THE TEXAS PRIMARY.

The Texas primary was a huge prize in the Democratic campaign of 2008, and Barack Obama's staffers spent fully $20 million to capture it—only to lose to Hillary Clinton. In the aftermath, Obama sat down with his key advisers for a postmortem.

Obama was calm and businesslike. There were no recriminations, just a quiet discussion of what had gone wrong and how to avoid those mistakes next time. At meeting's end, Obama stood up and walked toward the door. Then he turned around.

"I'm not yelling at you guys," he said.

He took another few steps and turned around again.

"Of course, after blowing through $20 million in a couple of weeks, I could yell at you. But…" (pause) "…I'm not yelling at you." With a quick laugh, Obama walked out.

Business life is full of such postmortems—as well it should be. If a company has no failures, it isn't taking enough risks. What counts is how you deal with mistakes—the lost account, the aborted new product, the competitor's move that blindsided you. Barack Obama's example in the wake of his Texas primary defeat is one to remember—cool to the core. And although "no drama Obama" may well be the inheritor of a genetic predisposition, psychologists say calmness can be a learned response.

Good leaders, whether they're engaged in politics or business, know there are times to cast blame and times to move on. If the problems in Texas had been caused by laziness, carelessness, or poor organization, Obama would surely have come down hard on the offenders. But if good-faith misjudgments, unforeseen developments, or plain bad luck were at fault, he knew it was better to blame nobody and focus on fixing the problems. The damage was done, but there were new battles to fight and no time or effort to be wasted in finger-pointing and staff shakeups. With no one singled out for blame, every adviser would feel a share of the responsibility—and all of them would work harder next time.

And Obama's abrupt parting laugh, showing how much the loss hurt, drove the message home.

BE COOL: PLAY HARDBALL WHEN YOU HAVE TO—LESSONS FROM A LIFETIME IN POLITICS.

Staying cool doesn't mean being a wuss. In his pickup basketball games, Obama is not above throwing an elbow under the basket—and in politics, much of his success has come from playing hardball. If an opponent is down, Obama is not about to let up.

His first campaign was a bid for a seat in the Illinois state senate. The incumbent, Alice Palmer, was giving it up to run for Congress, and she endorsed him. But when she lost her congressional race, she changed her mind and asked Obama to withdraw and give back her senate seat. By then, he had launched a campaign, recruited a staff, and attended countless neighborhood meetings. To Palmer's righteous fury, he refused to stand down.

When Palmer scrambled to get enough petition signatures to qualify for a spot on the ballot, Obama challenged many of her signatures—and a judge ruled enough of them invalid to end her bid. Still playing hardball, the Obama team went on to vet the petitions of the other two candidates, and he wound up as the only name on the ballot.

Soon, he was seen as one of the chamber's major players. He showed his talent for winning over conservatives by pushing through a bill cracking down on police officers who stopped more black drivers than white ones. His rationale was that it would protect Illinois from costly discrimination lawsuits, and his key tactic was patient listening and careful amendments to the bill to meet conservative objections. As his future U.S. Senate mentor Tom Daschle would say, he had learned that the "best way to persuade is with your ears."

In the presidential primary, Obama's toughest opponent was far and away Hillary Clinton, and his hardball strategy targeted her from the start. Once he had settled on his main theme of "change," said his adviser Larry Grisolano, the question became: "How do we talk about change in a way that makes Hillary Clinton pay a price for her experience?" The answer was to consistently describe her as a hardened pol who was more focused on working the system than on changing it. In a memo, Obama's advisers counseled him to phrase the characterization delicately, framing the election as a choice between "calculation" and "conviction," but not to "drive the contrasts so subtly … that the voters don't understand that we're talking about HRC."

In the general election, hardball was the game of choice against John McCain. McCain himself was a case study in the danger of letting an opponent recover. In the summer of 2007, his campaign had been written off as broke and floundering in internal chaos, but he regrouped and won the New Hampshire primary on his way to sweeping the Republican field.

So when it became clear that Obama's Web-based fundraising machine could reap unheard-of sums, the Illinois senator was quick to repudiate his pledge to abide by the limits of the public funding system. Obama paid a price for this apostasy in embarrassment and pointed criticism from McCain, but it was a small toll and more than offset by the flood of donations that flowed to his campaign coffers. In all, Obama raised an astonishing $639 million, nearly doubling McCain's $335 million. (It turned out to be an urban myth that most of Obama's money came from small contributors; in fact, just over a quarter was given by people whose contributions added up to $200 or less, though donations totaling $1,000 or more still made up a smaller slice than in the campaigns of McCain, John Kerry, and George Bush.) The overall result was a war chest that let Obama contest McCain even in states that seemed safely Republican, and McCain couldn't begin to match him.

Obama's advantage seemed so lopsided that he posted a warning about overconfidence in campaign headquarters, invoking his surprise defeat by Clinton in an early primary: "For those of you who are feeling giddy or cocky or think this is all set, I have just two words for you: New Hampshire." And he campaigned with all cylinders firing, never giving McCain so much as an instant to recover.

The lesson for business leaders is obvious, and well buttressed by experience: We have all seen cases of industry giants, complacent and prosperous, giving their competition an opening to fight back and take the lead. There was a time when AOL virtually owned the e-mail market, but it ignored the upstarts Google, Yahoo, and a host of others at its peril—and these days, AOL is a mid-pack player.

Wise leaders know they shouldn't lose their cool, but they must also never let up on their rivals— particularly when their company has an apparent advantage, because a lead can dry up in no time if a competitor finds a new angle or strikes a hidden chord that resonates with the customer. When your opponent is down, never let him up.

One CEO we know, who prefers to remain nameless, subscribes to that proposition. A skilled operations man, he plays hardball, for keeps. When he assumed the top spot at a major manufacturing company, it was floundering badly. He looked the situation over and rolled up his sleeves.

Most of his competitors were measuring themselves against a single benchmark: costs relative to revenues. But, as he knew, if everyone was using the same benchmarks, everyone was the same. So he and his leadership team began plotting every unit and every business function against those of its rivals. His goal was to become the best in every single category.

The exercise helped him successfully restructure his floundering enterprise. He was able to see clearly how his company stacked up against the competition, where it needed improvements, and where it needed to get tough and cut bait. His competitors were going to feel the heat.

A superior information-gathering network was one of the weapons Barack Obama used to surprise his competition, as Alice Jelin Isenberg discovered during the days she spent canvassing for Obama in New Hampshire. "I've been involved in a lot of campaigns," she told us, "but this was different." At the end of the day, as usual, canvassers reported back to the local headquarters and handed in their tallies. Out of, say, 100 households, maybe 60 people answered the door, and among them, maybe 30 said they were voting for Obama, 20 for McCain, and 10 no answers. The difference this time was that instead of the data just sitting there for sorting out at some point, the information Isenberg and the other canvassers gathered was instantly entered into "a young person's laptop" and dispatched to Obama headquarters in Chicago.

"This was happening in battleground states all around the country," she says. "The information was coming in from thousands of people like me. By 8:00 or 9:00 on a given night, the campaign knew how many people were for Obama. They didn't need pollsters."

Obama had another new tool to wield against his rival. In past campaigns, the "flushers"—volunteers assigned to round up nonvoters—had lists of people likely to vote their way, and they would go to the houses of these people to make sure they had voted. But the Obama campaign had found "Houdini," a program that let poll watchers identify voters in line and instantly remove them from the flushers' laptop lists, leaving only guaranteed nonvoters to be contacted.

The election-day drill was masterful. Where teams of volunteers had once assembled early in the day at shopping malls or union halls, they were now organized and rehearsed in advance. In the hard-fought state of Ohio alone, the Obama campaign spent six months recruiting and training 1,400 neighborhood teams. The national overseer of the program, Jon Carson, told a reporter, "We've taken the best of these volunteers, and they're giving us 40, 50, 60 hours a week. They're empowered, and we made them accountable." From his base in Chicago,

Carson said, he could be sure that the doors were being knocked on and the phone calls made.

As befits a hardball player, Barack Obama never lost his nerve. Late in the campaign, John McCain fluctuated in his response to the financial crisis, first announcing he would suspend his campaign to provide leadership in Washington, then failing to offer solutions and going back to the campaign trail. Obama held his own steady course, but his aides could portray McCain as a grandstanding opportunist. And with just days to go before the election, the Obama campaign spent $4 million to broadcast a half-hour infomercial in prime time on three national networks—a move McCain couldn't begin to match. On his knees, McCain never got up; Obama made sure of it.

Because he spoke softly and elegantly, because he was a Harvard graduate, some people had the impression that Obama was a kind of latter-day Adlai Stevenson, a sort of passive, see-all-sides-of-an-issue intellectual who could not possibly defeat such battle-tested candidates as Hillary Clinton and John McCain. In fact, Obama proved himself to be one tough character with a cool, calm demeanor that isn't easily shaken even in the thick of battle.

It's a model that works well in business, too. Playing hardball doesn't mean showboating; if you have power, there's no need to flaunt it. Too many business leaders make a habit of demanding the obeisance due a potentate. They rule by diktat, lording it over everyone, constantly trying to demonstrate their power and toughness by belittling those around them, delivering bellicose speeches, and making arbitrary decisions.

Aside from alienating everyone within reach of their voice or e-mail, such people are simply sowing the seeds of their own downfall. Leaders should know better. You play hardball when you have to, but otherwise you lead with reason and with empathy. Obama showed us how it can be done.

Be cool: Vent outside the tent— the lessons of Obama's pick-up basketball games.

We all know how politicians behave on the campaign trail: Talk, shake hands, kiss baby, and eat, eat, eat. Cannelloni in Little Italy, blintzes in Miami, sausage in Milwaukee, dim sum in Chinatown. Your average politician will always go whole hog for a vote, especially during a hard-fought race when appetites are fueled by stress.

But Barack Obama is not like most politicians. In both his primary and presidential runs, Obama maintained his abstemious attitude toward food. At a hamburger joint in Indiana, he nibbled on a single French fry. At a pancake house in Minnesota, he simply ordered flapjacks to go. Almost every night he ate the same dinner—salmon, rice, and broccoli.

Our president-elect is a very disciplined person who prides himself on maintaining a calm, cool, efficient exterior. Of course, he experiences feelings of frustration and anger like the rest of us; he just keeps them under wraps.

Unlike some of us, though, he also knows that beneath that cool, calm exterior lives something other than a saint in a well-tailored suit. He knows himself well enough to realize that he can lose his cool if he doesn't vent some of his feelings, so he schedules time for venting. Turns out that the trick to keeping his cool is to make time for losing it. Pickup basketball is his release valve, and he plays it hard. In the pickup game, there's no referee. Shirts get tugged, elbows get thrown, and every lay-up is hotly contested. The only rule: "No blood, no foul."

According to Craig Robinson, Obama's brother-in-law and the men's basketball coach at Oregon State University, the six-foot, two-inch Obama has good speed and endurance and a decent left-handed jump shot. He's too thin to muscle his way to the basket, but he has some tricky moves—a crossover dribble, for example—that can get him there. Robinson got to know Obama's game at his sister Michelle's behest. Michelle had Craig play one-on-one against her new boyfriend to see if he hogged the ball or called too many fouls.

Obama has it right. Too many people, particularly business leaders, spend all day, every day at their desks, with no time slotted for letting off steam. Then, when the steam does blow, they and everyone around them get burned. How often have you taken out your frustration over Major Screw-Up A on the perpetrator of Minor Screw-Up B? Or embarrassed yourself by throwing a tantrum over a weak project report?

The impact of such behavior goes well beyond its effect on you. It destroys office morale. Your staff becomes afraid to bring you bad news or to offer even the slightest criticism of your ideas. Potential new hires are put off by your reputation.

The truth is, we all need regular, routine, scheduled time when we can break away and vent the accumulated upsets and anger of the day. For some people it's night running, when the dark and relative silence are more conducive to letting the day's cares wash away and opening one's mind to big thoughts. Ryan Black, the CEO of Sambazon, the California-based maker of juice and sorbet made from Brazilian açai berries, packs up his surfboard and heads for the beach—usually nearby in Laguna or Huntington. But Black also makes time for extended stays in more exotic places like Nicaragua and Indonesia. There he leaves his business totally behind and does nothing but eat, sleep, and surf. Surfing helps him get away from his fast-paced career, Black told *Inc.* magazine.

One of the more unusual pursuits in this day and age is that of Michael Stelzer, whose day job keeps him behind a desk as president of a Missouri ad agency. When Stelzer wants to unwind, he fires up his backyard forge and sweats out his stress and frustration while banging away on a piece of red-hot metal. Stelzer has fashioned everything from deck railings to coat hooks, and he told *Advertising Age* that beating "the heck out" of a piece of metal is quite a stress reliever.

But exotic pastimes aren't required. Like Obama, you can use more traditional physical exercise—if not basketball, some other sport or the treadmill will do just fine. You can practice yoga or one of the other relaxation disciplines. Do whatever works for you. You, your family, and your friends will reap the benefits—and so will your company.

Be cool: Adjust to the moment—the lessons of Obama's South Carolina gaffe and Iowa recovery.

Barack Obama is certifiably cool, calm, and cerebral, yet, somewhat paradoxically, he is also seen as the best, most exciting public speaker of modern times. It was his electrifying keynote speech at the Democratic convention of 2004 that first gave him a place on the national stage. But until his 2008 campaign, his skills were formal and tailored to the grand scale. Unusual for a politician, he was inner-directed, guarded, and a bit remote—cool to the point of coming off as downright chilly. He lacked the ability to fire up his audience, to feed off their emotion and respond to it, to build a dialogue that could lift a crowd to a fever pitch of enthusiasm for him and his cause. It was a talent he would need, and he knew it; he was determined to learn.

An early experiment fizzled badly. As *Newsweek* told the story in its detailed chronicle of the 2008 race, Obama mimicked the call-and-response cadence used by black preachers as he tried to reassure an

African-American audience in South Carolina that a
black man could actually be elected president.

"I just want y'all to be clear…. I would not be
running if I weren't confident I was gon' *win*!" Obama
said. That triggered cheers, and cries of "Amen!"

"I'm not interested in *second* place!" The cheers
swelled as the crowd got into it.

"I'm not running to be *vice* president! I'm not
running to be *secretary* of something-or-other!" He
grinned as the crowd's energy poured back at him.
But carried away, he went a step too far, veering into
arrogant boasting.

"I was doing just fine before I started running for
president! I'm a United States senator already!"
The crowd went suddenly silent, but Obama forged
ahead. "Everybody already knows me! I already sold
a lot of books! I don't need to run for president to get
on television or on the radio…." A single shout broke
the silence, and Obama played his last, desperate
card: "I've been on *Oprah*!" That brought laughs and
cheers. He had squeaked through—but just barely.

Barack Obama, however, is a quick learner. Only a
week later, at a key dinner leading up to the Iowa
caucuses, he gave a typically eloquent speech to an

audience packed with his supporters. Then he came to the climax, a carefully rehearsed story of a dismal session in South Carolina with a small, bored crowd. One black woman had come to his rescue, leading the crowd in a counterpoint chant of "Fired Up!" and "Ready to Go!"

"So I've got one thing to ask you," Obama said to the dinner crowd, his voice rising to a near-shout. "Are you FIRED UP? Are you READY TO GO?" There was a mighty roar, and then the audience was chanting with him: "Fired up! Ready to go! FIRED UP! READY TO GO!" That became the windup of his standard stump speech from then on, and it always worked.

David Broder of *The Washington Post* described the unvarying scene: "As the shouting becomes almost too loud to bear, he adds the five words that capsulize his whole message and send the voters scrambling back into their winter coats and streaming out the door: 'Let's go change the world.'" In every audience, Broder wrote, "there is a jolt of pure electric energy at those closing words. Tears stain some cheeks—and some people look a little thunderstruck."

In your own business life, it's unlikely that you'll ever feel the vibes from a screaming, giant crowd in a stadium. But nearly everywhere you turn, there are electrifying signals being sent if only you can tune your antennae to receive them—signals from customers reacting to a marketing campaign, salesmen hearing a budget presentation, recruits in a training seminar.

To turn the inner feelings of your staff or customers into a zest for your product or a gung-ho attitude toward their jobs, you must watch for the person who lights up first and then catch that energy and reflect it back so the whole crowd of stakeholders can amplify it again and again.

Don't hesitate to deviate from your script to respond to a spark of enthusiasm and give your audience a chance to fan it into flame. Even a small meeting will get fired up if the impetus is a genuine emotion. But take care: You can't get this kind of response by giving someone a cue arranged in advance. Planned spontaneity has all the heat of those artificial fireplace logs that glow at the click of a switch.

Remember, too, that feedback encompasses far more than the reactions of a stirred-up crowd. It includes all the responses a leader gets from the people around him. Feedback is wherever you find it, and even when it isn't enthusiastic, good leaders constantly seek it.

FEEDBACK IS WHEREVER YOU FIND IT, AND EVEN WHEN IT ISN'T ENTHUSIASTIC, GOOD LEADERS CONSTANTLY SEEK IT.

When he was mayor of New York, Ed Koch was famous for asking everyone he met, "How'm I doin'?" Real leaders are also careful to listen more than they talk. A person skilled at listening makes anyone with an opinion feel like the biggest person in the room, because the responder's point of view is taken so seriously. And leaders who listen show that they understand the importance of their audience's response. John Whitehead, a former U.S. deputy secretary of state and co-chairman of the Goldman Sachs investment banking house, says, "When you talk, you are only saying what you already know, or think you know. You only learn when you listen."

It's also vital for a leader to make sure that the response he gets is as honest as possible, and the best way to do that is to avoid tipping his own hand as to which way he's leaning. Even good advisers are not above trying to win favor by telling the boss what they think he wants to hear, and they will be honest only if they can't figure that out. If you so much as hint at the conclusion you favor, all you'll hear from then on is the proof of why you're so right and so smart.

In nearly eight hours of meetings to discuss potential choices for Barack Obama's vice president, says Eric Holder, who headed the veep-vetting project and has since been tapped to be the new attorney general, Obama himself was patient and tireless. He brought up tiny details from the massive briefing reports on the candidates, and worked the room for feedback from every person there. If someone was silent for a while, Obama would single him out: "I haven't heard from you." But he never gave the slightest signal of his own preference down to the final choice of Delaware Senator Joe Biden. Says Holder: "You didn't know where he stood. I had a sense, but I didn't have any certainty." As a result, the advice was candid and the discussion probed all the pros and cons.

Staying cool under pressure, soliciting the opinions of others, and keeping an open mind until the final decision is made are all important attributes for a leader. But once the strategy is set and the way forward is determined, remember yet again: Stay focused on what matters, don't allow yourself to be distracted, and hold your course.

BE COOL: LEAD WITH HUMILITY—THE LESSONS OF ELECTION NIGHT.

The long campaign was finally over, and upward of 125,000 screaming, weeping fans were waiting in Chicago's Grant Park for President-Elect Barack Obama to claim his hard-won victory. Their mood was triumphant, some verging on gloating; they wanted nothing more than to hear Obama eviscerate the defeated Republicans.

But he stayed cool. His victory speech was quiet, conciliatory, a call for healing in a troubled time. "We are not enemies, but friends," he said simply, quoting Abraham Lincoln's First Inaugural Address. "Though passion may have strained, it must not break our bonds of affection." Some in the election-night crowd may have been disappointed, but the millions of Americans watching on national television saw just what kind of man they had voted for—someone who could rise above petty bickering and unite the country, a president who would actually bring modesty and humility to the Oval Office.

The invocation of Lincoln was no accident. Obama has long studied the 16th president and, like Lincoln, has often called humility an essential virtue. That doesn't mean meekness, submission, or the unctuousness of Charles Dickens' Uriah Heep. Humility is the sign of a leader confident enough to feel no need to swagger, boast, and dominate the people around him.

Apart from the Bible, Obama has cited Doris Kearns Goodwin's *Team of Rivals* as an essential book whose message will resonate with him as he prepares to move to the White House. It is the story of how Lincoln chose smart, ambitious, experienced political opponents as his closest advisers—men such as William Seward, who expected to control Lincoln as secretary of state but wound up as his greatest admirer and close friend. And in Obama's first appointments as president-elect, he has started along the same path.

STAYING COOL DOESN'T MEAN BEING A WUSS.

There's an important lesson in that for all of us: A truly effective leader doesn't crow about his or her victories, demand deference and unquestioning obedience, or spurn disagreement as disloyalty. That way lies the slippery slope to complacency and failure. A real leader reaches out to smart, opinionated people, learns from their arguments, and changes tactics without embarrassment when their ideas are better.

Think of Warren Buffett, the plain-spoken, multibillionaire Sage of Omaha whose decades of legendary achievement as an investor haven't dented his humility one whit. After a bad year, Buffett told his shareholders, "Overall, you would have been better off if I had regularly snuck off to the movies during market hours."

Humility does not come naturally to most business leaders, and you can be pardoned for resisting. You've worked hard to get where you are, looking forward to the day when you aren't going to be ordered about by people who consider themselves your betters. You have finally arrived at the top, and here we are advising you to be cool—to control the urge to take charge. We can only argue that humility will pay off, both in your relations with other people and your comfort in your own skin. A glance at the tin-pot despots of the world proves the case: Arrogance, pride, and constant domination are as exhausting as they are unattractive.

Some top executives show humility by taking over for employees who are absent or simply need a break. Shirley Ward, the founder and chief executive of the

$34 million Ward Group, a Dallas ad agency, fills in from time to time for the company's receptionist. When the position of media buyer fell vacant, she sat in there for a few weeks. Another Dallas executive, Chris McKee, managing partner of the $2 million accounting outsourcing firm, Venturity, shouldered some of the work of an assistant controller who had to go on sick leave.

The benefits of a management style based on humility are on prominent display at the Zingerman's community of businesses in Ann Arbor, Michigan. The tiny delicatessen that opened its doors in March 1982 on cobblestoned Detroit Street has metamorphosed into a $30 million empire with 545 employees, encompassing a bakehouse, a creamery, a roadhouse, a catering service, a consultancy, a wholesale coffee roasting business, a mail order operation—and, of course, a much-expanded version of that original deli.

The founders, Paul Saginaw and Ari Weinzweig, are still the bosses, though their definition of that role has evolved over the years. They believe in treating employees like customers. And as they make their rounds of the various businesses, they actively seek out ways they can help out.

"People give me assignments all the time," Weinzweig says. "Sometimes I'm the note-taker.

Sometimes I'm the cleaner-upper. Sometimes I bring food to the meetings."

The requests have to be reasonable. Occasionally, he admits, an employee will try to "take advantage" of their willingness to serve. But it doesn't happen often. And their humility has helped infuse employees with a strong sense of loyalty to them and their enterprise. It's no wonder that *Inc.* magazine has described Zingerman's as "the coolest small company in America."

Nowhere, however, is it written that humility must trump every other characteristic of the successful leader. Confidence and humility, for example, can co-exist comfortably. Witness Barack Obama, who can be so confident that he seems cocky. When he was interviewing Patrick Gaspard before hiring him as his political director, Obama warned: "I think that I'm a better speechwriter than my speechwriters. I know more about policies on any particular issue than my policy directors. And I'll tell you right now that I'm gonna think I'm a better political director than my political director." Yet Obama also knows when he has overstepped. Conservative columnist Peggy Noonan once criticized him for having compared his own early struggles to "Lincoln's rise from poverty, his ultimate mastery of language and law, [and] his capacity to overcome personal loss and

remain determined in the face of repeated defeat."
Noonan wrote cuttingly that Obama was "explaining
that he's a lot like Abraham Lincoln, only sort of
better." Recounting the exchange in his memoir,
The Audacity of Hope, Obama wrote wryly: "Ouch!"

His sense of confidence shows in his appointments
for high-level jobs in his administration. His choices
have included some high-powered, strong-minded
people—a far cry from the calm, even-tempered sort
he chose as campaign aides. It takes a self-assured
person to choose Rahm Emanuel, a famously rough-
and-tough congressman, as your chief of staff, for
example, and Hillary Clinton as your secretary of
state. It says that you want to hear disparate points
of view—and you're confident you can take the heat
and make your own calls.

For Obama, humility includes maintaining the
appearance of modesty, as he showed in the
campaign after the McCain forces, sensing a
vulnerability, attacked him as a mere "celebrity"
akin to Paris Hilton or Britney Spears. As early as the
primaries, says his senior adviser Anita Dunn, the
campaign diagnosed a "rally problem": While Hillary
Clinton earnestly worked small-town crowds and
town-hall meetings, Obama's mass appeal drew vast
crowds to rallies that dramatized his oratory but did
nothing to bolster his ordinary-guy credentials. The

campaign set up a "presumptuous watch" that kept celebrity endorsers at arm's length and toned down the bombast and glitz of a Hollywood-style setting for Obama's acceptance speech at the Democratic National Convention in Denver.

At bottom, however, Obama's humility isn't just for show—it is real, his confidence tempered by relentless self-appraisal. For example, after participating in a 2007 health-care forum with Hillary Clinton, someone whom Obama genuinely respects, he realized that she had outshone him. "She was very good, and I need to meet that standard, meet that test," *The New Yorker* quoted him as telling his chief strategist, David Axelrod. "I am not a great candidate now, but I am going to figure out how to be a great candidate."

Whether it's a politician like Obama or a business leader like Zingerman's Ari Weinzweig, the willingness to put pride and the trappings of power aside can produce great results. We are not suggesting that you give up your decision-making role or that you somehow grovel before your employees. What we are suggesting is that, in your daily contacts with your people, you show them that you don't take yourself too seriously, that you are truly interested in hearing their point of view, and that you want to help them work in any way you can. A little humility on your part can go a long way toward building a cooperative, enthusiastic workforce.

P.S. At one point, Obama's victory speech in Chicago's Grant Park was scheduled to end with fireworks. Obama called them off. Talk about cool.

Nothing is less useful in a crisis than a leader addicted to tantrums, accusations, and denunciations. That's not leadership; it's idiocy and weakness, guaranteed to turn minor disputes into major wars.

Just as Barack Obama shrugged off underhanded attacks with an almost other-worldly calm, business leaders need to handle bad news and unexpected setbacks with personal composure and organizational credibility. This requires taking time to prepare for any surprise with sound contingency plans, readiness to execute those plans, and willingness to act first rather than blame first.

"...AT THE END OF THE DAY, YOU CAN'T HIDE WHO YOU ARE."
—DAVID AXELROD

Obama won over voters by seeming presidential. Business leaders can win over their own constituents by meeting the test of staying unflappable in all crises, major or minuscule. Admirable behavior evokes admiring reactions—hard work, devotion, loyalty. Needless to say, the coolest leader invariably attracts the most effective followers and builds the most efficient organization. An old saying has it that wars can be lost for want of a horseshoe nail. In business, whole marketing campaigns, bottom lines, and share prices can depend on the leader never once losing his or her temper.

Staying cool, of course, isn't the only requirement for succeeding, in business or in politics. These days, you must also know how to make use of new techniques and tools, especially social technologies—as Barack Obama did in his campaign, and as we'll discuss in the next chapter.

LESSONS

- ▶ Ignore the sideshows—keep your eye on the center ring.

- ▶ Fix the problem; forget the blame.

- ▶ Play hardball when necessary.

- ▶ Vent outside the tent.

- ▶ Adjust to the moment.

- ▶ Lead with humility.

BUSINESS—
LIKE POLITICS—
IS EXTREMELY
PERSONAL.

CHAPTER 3
Be Social

Not least of Obama's victory secrets was his agile use of social networking—using Web sites like Facebook, Flickr, Twitter, and YouTube that spurred millions of young Americans not only to register as first-time voters, but also to help make sure everyone got to the polls. Obama capitalized on Internet technologies hardly imagined in the last presidential election—blogs, texting, cell-phone networks, and an entire coast-to-coast grassroots community (My. BarackObama.com). These tools created instant communication with his supporters, turning small donors into a mighty army of contributors and volunteers, while adding ever more crucial electoral votes in battleground states.

Obama's use of social technologies had the double-whammy effect of turning excited individuals into a nationwide crusade. For example, his iPhone application ("Obama 08") converted the user's own electronic address book into an electioneering tool—a list of priority phone calls to friends in battleground states and other key areas. With a few thumb clicks, Obama supporters thus canvassed their own friends in the most cost-efficient way, vastly multiplying the Obama campaign's reach while conserving money.

Twitter became an electronic poll-watcher for Obama on Election Day. Prodding and texting each other live all day, Twitter's avid Obama microbloggers made sure no one failed or forgot to vote. Facebook users checked a box on their page to show friends they had done their civic duty. By 10:30 Eastern time on election night, the Facebook voter tally alone hit 4.9 million—a barometer of healthy democracy unprecedented in presidential campaigning.

IN BUSINESS AS IN POLITICS, ONLINE COMMUNITIES ARE MAKING OUR USUAL, ESTABLISHED WAYS OF DOING THINGS PASSÉ.

For businesses, the benefits of using these technologies are obvious—everything from lower costs to more customers, greater efficiency, and bigger profits. Following the Obama-inspired guidelines laid out in this chapter will almost certainly benefit your company, but only if you also strive to overcome a serious business problem that we call CSD (corporate social dysfunction). After helping hundreds of leaders think about social technologies, we have found all too many are afflicted with CSD's primary symptoms—egotism and a reluctance to relinquish control to their communities, be it customers, employees, or partners.

CSD also infects its victims with the false impression that business is not personal. Wrong. As the opening of this chapter suggests, business—like politics—is extremely personal. Work and its contentments, as well as its discontents, are shot through with emotions. People fired from their jobs feel a personal grievance. People supported by their companies feel gratitude. And customers become loyal when they can share a corporation's goals and feel that their use of its products helps improve the world. The reality is that the more personal a business is in a positive sense, the more valuable and resilient (and profitable) it becomes.

Here's what we can learn from campaign Obama.

BE SOCIAL: CULTIVATE THE NEW GRASSROOTS, THE NETROOTS—THE LESSONS OF TAKING ON THE INCUMBENTS.

On November 5, 2006, Barack Obama called a meeting of his closest advisers in the Chicago offices of political consultant David Axelrod, Obama's chief campaign strategist. The day before, the Democratic

Party had achieved a sweeping victory over the Republicans, seizing control of the Senate, the House of Representatives, and most of the governorships and state legislatures. Obama chose this moment to chart the strategy he intended to pursue in his run for the Democratic nomination.

Along with Axelrod, Obama's audience that day included his wife Michelle, his campaign manager David Plouffe, soon-to-be communications director Robert Gibbs, and long-time counselors Marty Nesbitt and Valerie Jarrett.

The setting was unremarkable—a small, badly lit conference room provisioned with bottles of water, soda cans, and cookies. Obama's presentation made up for it. His message was nothing less than revolutionary. The country was ready for change, he said—not just a change of administration, but a change away from politics as usual. His chief opponent in the primary, Hillary Clinton, was sure to have an early lock on the big-money donors and the backing of most party leaders. His heart and his head told him that he should travel a new and dramatically different route.

His campaign, he said, would be "ground up, rather than top down." When he was a political organizer,

Obama had seen how a grassroots campaign could succeed. He had brought change to the mean streets of Chicago, once registering 150,000 new voters using just ten staffers and 700 volunteers. Now he could do the same for the nation as a whole.

Beyond that, though, Obama and his aides had to acknowledge Clinton's head start. The grassroots approach was basically Obama's only option, a necessity if he was going to overtake her. But it would not be simply an old-fashioned, knock-on-every-door kind of campaign. No, the grassroots Obama particularly wanted to target would be found on the Internet—social media and user-generated content in particular. If he could sell his message of change to the online millions, he could build a formidable campaign chest and mobilize a dedicated army of workers.

Obama recognized that he had no choice: He had to become intimately involved with, and dependent on, the electronic grassroots, or *netroots*, a term coined to describe political activism worked through online social media. Today, that necessity holds just as true for every business leader, whether or not you realize it. In business as in politics, online communities are making our usual, established ways of doing things passé.

For instance, it's been obvious for a while now that traditional marketing doesn't work very well. The public doesn't trust companies to tell them the truth about their products. They ignore half of TV commercials, and if they have digital video recorders such as TiVo, they skip over the ads altogether. A direct-mail campaign that gets a two percent response is considered a great success. Studies show that most consumers, when asked whom they look to for reliable product information, reply, "A person like me."

In the past, that meant Mabel or Mo were likely to talk with a family member or a neighbor before making a big purchase. The difference now: They look online.

Almost overnight, it seems, the Internet has become the place where billions of people of every age, rank, and ethnicity hang out, where decisions are made about what to think, where to go, what to buy—the Net has become part clubhouse, part library, part multiplex, part shopping mall. In the United States alone, more than half the population watched at least one online video in 2008. A third of us regularly research health issues on social-networking sites. Facebook counts over 100 million registered members.

This immense grassroots community is transforming the way business is conducted. Individually and on social-networking sites, its members compare notes about products they own or hope to own. How long before they break down? How much noise do they make? Is there anything cheaper? This is where Mabel and Mo decide what to buy, not sitting in front of their television.

Functions that were once the sole province of marketers are being usurped by people online. They research competing brands to find the best deal and spread the word for all to see. They sell each other on one product or another. They provide customer support, answering questions about product performance and solving problems.

The following vignettes show just how much user-based Internet marketing programs have changed the business landscape:

- ▶ *Evolution,* a thought-provoking mini-film produced for Dove, Unilever's line of soaps and hygiene products, was cited as a sterling example of the new kind of marketing by Jonah Berger, a Wharton marketing professor. The video spot, which lasts only 1 minute and 14 seconds, went viral in 2007, getting almost

5.5 million views on YouTube. It's a time-lapse sequence showing how a plain-looking model morphs into a sexy billboard face, thanks to an army of make-up artists and doctoring with Photoshop. It ends with the comment, "No wonder our perception of beauty is distorted."

Is this designed to sell soap? No, says Berger: "It's about more than hawking soap"; it's about "starting a dialogue about beauty that Dove is a part of." The film is just one element of Dove's Campaign for Real Beauty, explains Kathy O'Brien, Dove's marketing director. The promotion includes advertising, Web sites, billboards, real-world events, and a charitable Self-Esteem Fund. It has been wildly successful: More than 4.5 million people "have visited Campaignforrealbeauty.com and shared words of encouragement supporting the efforts to widen the narrow definition of beauty," O'Brien reports.

By identifying itself with a noble cause and then inspiring the crowd to spread that fact far and wide, Dove has planted the seeds of customer approval that it will harvest eventually in the form of increased sales.

▶ A wholly unconventional two-minute video created by a professional comedy trio was chosen as one of ten semifinalists in a YouTube contest sponsored by Toyota's 2009 Corolla. Here's the gist: Three college guys are on a road trip to Daytona Beach, Florida, for spring break. The guy in the backseat casually announces that he has brought along a bard. His friends up front peer back to see two musicians in Elizabethan dress, one holding a tambourine, the other a recorder. "A bard?" the buddies ask. "Yeah," says the backseat guy. "He sings about our deeds and adventures and stuff. My family got one when we went skiing in Vail; it's pretty sweet." Several seconds of inane singing follow as the car's driver begins to get annoyed. Eventually, he gets pulled over for speeding as the spot ends.

By traditional marketing standards, the spot is a disaster. Not only does it never even mention a Toyota Corolla, but the kids are actually driving a Honda. "How do you make the Corolla seem irreverent?" asks Wharton's Berger, before answering his own question: "You can't fake that; you actually have to be that way."

Toyota spokeswoman Cindy Knight explained that the payoff wasn't the actual winning spot, but the contest itself: The company is "trying to develop a relationship with the next generation of Corolla buyers," a group she defined as young, well-educated consumers who are natives of the online world and heavily involved with YouTube. *The Wall Street Journal* reported that Toyota's YouTube campaign cost $4 million and involved intense collaboration among the social-networking site, Google, Toyota, and Saatchi & Saatchi, the advertising agency hired by the carmaker. The contest served its purpose by getting the crowd involved, both as creators of the entries and as the source of blogs and e-mails about them.

▶ A brilliant campaign by Sprint Nextel and Suave, another Unilever brand, created a vast online community of mothers—and a sea of invaluable user-generated content—by asking them to contribute funny stories about being a mom. The best of the bunch were produced into a series of Webisodes and cross-promoted on *The Ellen DeGeneres Show*. The campaign, "In the MotherHood," got online contributions from tens of thousands of moms and was called "surprisingly successful" by *Adweek* magazine. "What we ended up building was not just entertainment, but also an area where mothers can dialogue with each other," explained Ted Moon, director of digital marketing at Sprint Nextel. Mothers, he said, clearly felt a need for membership in a community, and "being associated with bringing that [about] provided great gains for us as a company."

BE SOCIAL: CREATE A SEAMLESS COMMUNITY—THE LESSONS OF MY.BARACKOBAMA.COM.

In February 2007, Barack Obama made a decision that would turn out to be key to his run for the presidency: He hired Chris Hughes.

When word got out that the sandy-haired, baby-faced Hughes—who looks even younger than his 24 years—was joining the campaign, it created a stir in some quarters. The addition of Hughes meant that Obama was going to expend major energy and resources to build a breakthrough Internet presence.

Hughes was raised in Hickory, North Carolina, and moved north to attend Phillips Academy in Andover, Massachusetts, before going on to Harvard University. At Harvard, he roomed with computer prodigy Mark Zuckerberg. Together with a couple of friends, the pair created an open-access Web site where Harvard students could connect with each other. The site rapidly expanded to include any university student, then any high school student, then anyone 13 and older. Today, what is now known as Facebook has more than 100 million active users.

IN EVERY INTERACTION WITH THE ONLINE MASSES, OBAMA'S AIDES SOUGHT TO BUILD A RELATIONSHIP IN WHICH THE MASSES WERE IN CHARGE.

Hughes quit his executive post at Facebook to join the Obama campaign (though he continues to hold stock options worth many millions of dollars). After settling into his tiny cubicle at the candidate's headquarters in Chicago, he fashioned a new Web site called My.BarackObama.com, known within the campaign as MyBo. MyBo was the place you landed if you indicated on the barackobama.com main site that you wanted to help get Obama elected.

In ways clear, elegant, and entertaining—its design was often compared to that of the iPod and other Apple products—MyBo encouraged and enabled more than a million visitors to donate their time and/or cash to the cause. The site's enormous power derived from the fact that visitors, after they understood their options, were basically on their own. And as Hughes says in comparing MyBo to Facebook, "What's really similar and fascinating is that they are both powered by people."

À la Facebook and other social-networking sites, MyBo members created their own personal pages and joined congenial groups, supplying the usual personal information and photograph. But besides sharing their info, MyBo members were expected to commit to campaign activities with their group, such as phoning a list of people provided by the site. They were also expected to generate an "activity index" on their page and report the results of their efforts to date, while also setting up a personal fundraising page that included their individual dollar goal and a message to be sent to friends and family. Each person's page included a thermometer to show his or her progress toward that goal, and visitors to a page could see the results, too—a not very subtle form of peer pressure.

Hughes's handiwork raised hundreds of millions of dollars for Obama, inspired millions of phone calls, organized tens of thousands of events, and is widely acknowledged as a major factor in the election's outcome. A blogger offered this critique: "You have to love a story about a 24-year-old who made a monumental difference by helping Barack Obama to become president of the United States. In other words, this young dude helped change the world." He also showed how the social-networking model can be used to promote and raise money for a new political brand.

The first goal of a business-oriented social network, of course, is to amass a collection of people who have a stake in your company and its products. Chris Hughes had an easier task in that regard because the potential members of his network were self-selected Obama supporters. But every company has a substantial pool of people to draw upon—satisfied customers and investors, employees, ex-employees, all of their relatives, and residents of the communities in which a company's plants are located.

Just as Barack Obama did with My.BarackObama. com, a company can attract people to its social network by promoting it on the company's main Web site. But easing your way into building a community is like flinching your way into cold seawater. Plunging is actually easier. So our advice is, just go for it.

Business leaders tend to get into social media one step at a time—beginning with a discussion forum, say, or perhaps a blog. That's easy enough, and the inexpensive way to do it is to cobble the technologies together on your own. But that approach creates a problem: When you want to take the next step, the two parts might not connect seamlessly. A member of the discussion forum, for instance, might have to register again to read blogs and then can't just skip back and forth between the two areas. It's cumbersome and off-putting, and you, as the host, can't easily retrieve and use information the members provide.

It's better to start by building an integrated community platform that can support all your potential activities. You can hire a software services provider to do the building, or, if you have the skills and energy, you can build the platform yourself. The point is this: However you create it, a seamless platform is far better than a cobbled-together contraption.

When your platform is in place, you have a launch pad to several other activities. Members who register for your discussion forum, let's say, can automatically sign on for other things, like rating products or posting comments to a blog. These members will also be available for a survey, and when you get around to creating a wiki, your members can contribute to that, too.

And when the host (that would be you) is using an integrated platform, you will have access to far more information than you get with disparate tools. In a discussion group, for example, you can set up a key-word search that tells you the ten most frequently used words in a conversation. You can look at all the discussions the group has had and find which of them are most frequently read and which products are most highly rated or which are most often listed as favorites.

OBAMA SOUGHT TO BUILD A STRONG, ONGOING RELATIONSHIP WITH THE ONLINE COMMUNITIES.

For the Obama campaign, the MyBo social-networking platform became a giant electronic megaphone to disseminate the candidate's message. E-mails containing his positions were dispatched to each member, turning viral as they skipped from one site to another across the Internet. And in urging members to make phone calls to raise cash and/or get out the vote, Hughes made sure they were provided with scripts to use, a technique aimed at maintaining a positive image for the campaign and eliciting the best response from those receiving calls.

The ways in which a seamless social network can benefit its sponsor are essentially a function of the ingenuity and dedication of its members, which is to say, infinite. Here are two examples from members' fundraising pages on MyBo as of July 2007: Andrew Nicholas, a Denver teacher, brought in more than $1,200 for Obama by asking people to contribute according to their height; Emily Stanton, a homemaker in Baltimore, raised $744 by soliciting donations for Obama from people who agreed to sponsor her as she trained for her first marathon.

By using a seamless platform, the Obama campaign stayed true to the candidate's community-organizing roots: It sought to get across a strong sense of mission while drawing in a broad group of people, many of them young, who had previously felt somewhat disenfranchised from the political process.

BE SOCIAL: NURTURE YOUR LISTS— THE LESSONS OF CHANGE.COM.

When the votes were all cast and counted, the measure of Barack Obama's Internet triumph could be found in the numbers. My.BarackObama.com had 1.5 million members, sorted into 35,000 groups according to geography, vocation, and shared interests like "favorite band." The site's members had organized 150,000 campaign-related events and raised a large chunk of the $639 million in contributions to the campaign. They had also responded to a plea from the Obama camp to contribute to a fund for hurricane victims, bringing in a substantial sum.

With a track record like that, the next question for Obama and his team after the election became: What do we do with all those people, that huge band of dedicated online supporters? And what about those other millions of people who went to the rallies and handed over their phone numbers and e-mail addresses, and manned the phone centers and knocked on doors and ran cookie sales on Obama's behalf? Both groups, 4 million people according to some counts, had become accustomed to receiving e-mails and text messages from the candidate, his top aides, and his family. What now?

Like previous political Web sites, the huge endeavor might have ended with a simple "thanks for the memories" when the campaign was over. But not this time. A new Web site was created, Change.com, and the president-elect kept those e-mails and text messages coming. Obama evidently intended to stay in touch over the long haul, and it seemed certain that he would find ways to mobilize his millions of already ardent admirers—and as many more as he could sign up—to advance his programs. After all, these people were more than just fans; they were looking for ways to make things better in America— and Obama was likely to have some ideas about that after he settled into the Oval Office.

The proximate rationale for Change.com was to keep supporters abreast of Obama's appointments and other initiatives during the transition period by means of a blog and copies of press releases. But the site also maintains its participatory flavor. Under the heading "America Serves," for example, there's a short list of the new service organizations Obama intends to create, including help for underserved schools and work in clinics and hospitals. There's a form to fill out if you're interested in volunteering.

As we were going to press with this book, former Senator Tom Daschle—chosen to become secretary of health and human services in the Obama administration—announced that several thousand people had posted comments on health on the Web site, and that he plans a conference call with 1,000 picked supporters who will weigh in on how to restructure the health-care system. Daschle will stay in touch with the community via online videos, blogs, and e-mail alerts.

Front and center on the site is a box urging visitors to express their opinions about the country's direction: "Share your experiences and your ideas—tell us what you'd like the Obama-Biden administration to do and where you'd like the country to go." The e-mail and snail-mail addresses of all respondents are no doubt added to that mammoth campaign list, as are those of people who accept the site's invitation to apply for a job in the new administration.

It's an obvious caveat that very few companies will gain the kind of admiration and dedication so many social networkers developed for Obama. But fervency isn't essential to business gains. Nike, for one, is taking a shot with its nikeplus.com social-networking site, and it appears to be connecting by working its own worldwide lists of runners—and, soon, basketball players.

The technology behind the site is an application called Nike+ that records a runner's pertinent information so long as he or she is wearing a Nike+ wristwatch-like sports band or carrying an iPod Nano device. Sensors in the wristband or the iPod can be popped out and inserted into specially designed Nike shoes that then track speed, mileage, and calories burned with every stride.

When a runner removes the linking device from her shoe, she can access nikeplus.com by connecting the band device to her computer or by docking her iPod. All of a runner's run and race results and workout data are stored on the site and can be accessed at any time. Runners can set personal goals and see how fast they are progressing, or perhaps challenge friends to match their efforts.

Since nikeplus.com's launch in 2006, runners have uploaded stats covering more than 97 million miles, and Nike's share of running-shoe sales has risen from 48 percent to 61 percent of the overall market, according to *BusinessWeek*. When the Ballers Network is up and running, Nike also hopes to attract basketball players with a Facebook application that will let hoopsters manage their teams online while organizing games in the real world. But to us, the possibilities for bringing to the Nike networking site participants in all kinds of sports would appear to be endless. Why couldn't Nike equip its golf, tennis, cycling, walking, or any other sports shoe with its tracking technology?

The success of both Obama and Nike in adapting strategies to changed circumstances, along with the Obama campaign's determination not to lose touch with the president's communities, should resonate with every business leader. If Nike is any indication, and we think it is, these days of economic malaise are no time to abandon online communities. If you have a following on one or more social networking sites, we urge you to hold on to it and expand it if you can. In today's business world, social networkers are the coin of the realm, the means by which you can achieve growth and profitability—if only you will give the sites sufficient resources and strong leadership, inspiring the online crowd to work in your behalf.

Having won the job he sought, Obama could easily
have closed down his complex communications
network or taken some half-hearted step to stay
connected to his troops. He had a lot on his mind,
facing the most intractable set of problems in
generations. But he, of all people, understands the
power of the online grassroots to move mountains,
so he not only held on but also expanded his
networking. Businesspeople should make the same
choice, and for the same reason.

BE SOCIAL: LET YOUR NETROOTS GROW INTO EVERY CREVICE—THE LESSONS OF FACEBOOK (AND MYSPACE, LINKEDIN, TWITTER, DIGG, AND SCRIBD).

A couple of weeks before Barack Obama was
proclaimed president-elect of the United States, he
won another title, Marketer of the Year. At the annual
conference of the Association of National Advertisers
in Orlando, Florida, Obama beat out Apple and
Zappos, Nike and Coors. My.BarackObama.com
came in for particular praise.

But the social-networking strategy of the Obama
camp extended far beyond his site. His image and
message were everywhere on the Internet. Much of
what was seen and heard on such sites as Facebook,

MySpace, LinkedIn, Twitter, Digg, and Scribd were
of the Obama team's design, but the content was
designed to fit each individual site and its viewers.

For Facebook, the team created an application
called "Obama" that encompassed all of the content
produced by the campaign, including videos, press
releases, and blogs. It even allowed users to rate the
media, highlighting the most popular pieces. The
application attracted a million regular supporters.
Of course, the Obama team had a certain advantage
when designing for Facebook, because, as we
mentioned earlier, Chris Hughes, a co-founder of the
site, was working for the campaign.

More and more companies are discovering the
advantages of tapping into social-networking sites
that were once the sole province of your friends.
And the successful ones understand that it's not a
one-size-fits-all proposition. Different sites appeal to
different folks.

The Coca-Cola Company, for instance, has attracted
a broad following on Facebook, where numerous
fans pay homage to "the real thing" with sites they've
created themselves. But Graco Children's Products
decided that a blog would work best for the young-
parent crowd it seeks to attract. And Comcast found

Twitter to be just right for reaching out to customers with complaints.

As for Coca-Cola, it's happy to let its fans sing its praises in any way they choose. And, according to *The Atlanta Journal-Constitution*, it tries not to intrude with its own sales pitches and the like, preferring to let users of the network dictate how much interaction they want.

Brian Uzzi, at Northwestern University's Kellogg School of Management, applauds Coke's insight. Too much butting in and online fans can start reacting the same way people do to telemarketers who call at dinnertime, he says. They can turn against a company they once supported and might even start a negative blog about it.

We believe marketers should think of online communities as private places (even though they're anything but) and wait to be invited into the crowd's living room for a conversation of the host's choice.

Graco, the maker of children's car seats, high chairs, and the like, tries to take that softer, non-annoying approach with its blog.gracobaby.com, where parents come together to talk about common problems and ask questions such as whether sippy cups are bad for a toddler's tooth development, writes *Journal-Constitution* reporter Peralte Paul. Sure, the company views the site as a way to market its brand and image, but it prefers to begin by making visitors comfortable with Graco and its products and then develop long-term product loyalty through helpful discussions about parenting issues.

Though Comcast is happy with its Twitter connection, its initial experience with social media via YouTube was not so gratifying. The cable company felt the sting when YouTubers were treated to a videotape of one of its technicians fast asleep on a customer's couch after waiting for more than an hour to get a response from his own company. To Comcast's never-ending embarrassment, the video was viewed 1.28 million times.

But all's well that end's well, and the feedback from YouTube and the blogosphere prompted Comcast to fix its customer service by adding thousands of new reps. From there it went on to start its Comcastcares account on Twitter to address customer complaints and answer questions; it has gotten nearly 12,000 "tweets." Now a newly enlightened Comcast sings the praises of the blogosphere, calling it a great place to get valuable feedback from customers who might not otherwise let the company know they're having problems.

Visa has gotten into social networking, too, using it as a way to reach small businesses. But rather than trying to build an online community of its own, the company took advantage of one ready-made—Facebook—to launch its Visa Business Network. "We wanted to go where small businesses are already going online," said the company's head of small-business marketing. And to promote its new venture, Visa turned to—what else?—social networking. The company used some traditional print and online media ads, but the bulk of its advertising consisted of ads that appeared in Facebook users' news feeds and in blog content.

It should come as no surprise that Facebook advertising proved extremely efficient in targeting and attracting new users. After all, that's where the users Visa was targeting hang out. Within a matter of months, the Visa Business Network could count 21,000 small-business profiles on its site, exceeding its expectations.

Perhaps the root cause of netroots' efficiency is its users' penchant for letting you know quickly what they like and don't like. Chris Hughes knows that, which is why he made sure that the Obama material dispatched to any given site was carefully tailored to the interests of its members. Twitter, for instance, lets members stay in touch throughout the day with frequent short blogs. When the candidate's energy plan was ready, quick status updates sent to Twitter let users know that they could read the plan at Obama's Web site. A copy of the plan was also dispatched to Scribd.com, a document-sharing site, to be added to Obama's profile there. On LinkedIn.com, a site dedicated to helping members network, Obama initiated discussions about the future of U.S. business. On SecondLife.com, the Internet's most popular virtual world, the "Obama for President" group sponsored a music festival to raise cash for the campaign.

Hundreds of videos, produced rapidly and cheaply by the Obama staff, were put up on YouTube. Toward the end of the campaign, they were being uploaded at the rate of 20 or more a day. As of October 2008, the videos had been seen 77 million times on YouTube alone.

When it wasn't feeding customized messages to the networking sites, the Obama team was asking its volunteers to do so. A volunteer who signed up at MySpace, for example, might be urged to put an Obama bumper sticker on her page. On Digg.com, members post everything from news items to videos, and the postings that win the most votes appear on the site's front page. An Obama volunteer who dug Digg might have been asked to post an article that knocked John McCain or praised Obama.

The organizational and technological skills exhibited
in the campaign were simply amazing. Alice Jelin
Isenberg, a member of Obama's New England
Steering Committee, told us that her group was
bombarded with e-mails, three to five a day, from all
branches of the campaign—local, state, and national.
The multi-front network assault allowed the Obama-
Biden forces to outflank their opponents in terms of
fundraising, canvassing, phone contacts—you name
it. (The fundraising success was due in no small part
to the New England committee; the Massachusetts
volunteers raised more money per capita than any
other state.)

"The field organization knew its job," Isenberg said.
"The weekend before the election, I kept getting
e-mails asking if I was going to New Hampshire? Or
was I going to be making phone calls from Boston?
They knew what every volunteer was doing." So by
Election Day, the campaign was so well organized
that every hand knew exactly what to do.

Dorothy Terrell, another member of the New England
committee, was boggled by the near-constant e-mail
communication—especially the one that arrived
just before Barack Obama went on stage to make his
victory speech at Grant Park. President-Elect Obama
was so engaging, and his supporters so dedicated,
that some thought his e-mails were meant just for
them, Terrell told us.

The e-mails continue to this day, keeping the troops at the ready to lend support. It's "very smart" to continue using online social media, Terrell declares. And she's right, especially because the talented Obama team is so good at connecting with people in a variety of ways.

Business leaders are, of course, totally familiar with the notion of tailoring marketing messages for different audiences in the offline world, but they've been slow to apply that approach in working with social networks. Most organizations now have their own Web sites, but they have been wary of embracing the netroots concept of promoting their message and their products through blogs, podcasts, wikis, and other social media outlets. They recognize that the rules of those roads are different, and they're not sure they have a license to drive on all of them.

ON A SOCIAL NETWORKING SITE, A COMPANY IS JUST ANOTHER VISITOR— AND NOT NECESSARILY A WELCOME ONE.

Like the public as a whole, members are suspicious of business, and they're also protective of their site.

Representatives of your company need to behave in
a friendly, straightforward way. Your page should be
informative and engaging in a manner that appeals
to the particular audience you're trying to reach.
Finding the right tack between entertaining and
promoting is a challenge, but it's one we believe
must not be ignored. As Obama has shown, the
opportunities for promoting a brand on the social-
networking sites are, well, virtually infinite.

Be social: Arm yourself against, and don't take, cheap shots—the lessons of "Hillary Clinton (D-Punjab)."

The Democratic primary campaign was in full cry.
In the press, on television, and especially online, the
candidates and their staffers were tossing grenades
back and forth. It was politics as usual, but Barack
Obama was disturbed by the steady increase in
personal attacks. Why is it, he wondered, that you're
expected to "bomb the hell out of someone" to prove
how tough you are? There should be some limits.

Then one of his own staffers went too far. In a
press release, the aide described Hillary Clinton as
"(D-Punjab)" instead of "(D-New York)"—a snide
reference to Clinton's longtime support of India.
Obama was already concerned about how the public

viewed his campaign's treatment of the former first lady. Their relationship had deteriorated badly since that day, soon after he announced his candidacy, when she refused his handshake on the Senate floor, and he knew that a primary campaign isn't forever; if he won, he would need her help to beat the Republicans.

Obama called a staff meeting and voiced his objections to the swipe against Clinton. He understood that his team wanted to insulate him from the press release sniping, and therefore nobody had run it past him. But the cheap shots had to end. "I'm saying this loud and clear—no winks, no nods here," he declared. "I'm looking at every one of you. If you think you're close to the line, the answer isn't to protect me—the answer is to ask me."

In business as in politics, negative marketing has been on the rise—though in business, the proximate cause has been the economic downturn. In hard times, what practitioners like to call "comparative advertising"—freely translated as "blast the competition"—is traditionally a favorite tactic.

In October 2008, Dunkin' Donuts fired the opening salvo in a campaign against Starbucks with an ad showing a group of tasters preferring Dunkin' Donuts coffee to Starbucks. The negative tone of the campaign was established with the name of the Web site created for the occasion: dunkinbeatstarbucks. com. On the site, you're given a chance to send an online card to your address list with such messages as "friends don't let friends drink Starbucks."

One problem with negative campaigns is that they invite a response. That's what happened when Campbell's Soup promoted a new variety, Select Harvest, with an ad slamming Progresso because its soups had such ingredients as monosodium glutamate. In one ad, Progresso chicken noodle was shown with a headline, "Made With MSG," while beside it, the headline on a Select Harvest chicken noodle was "Made With TLC."

Progresso responded with one set of ads promising to remove MSG from its soups. In the other set, a taste test between the two brands ends with Progresso the clear winner.

A spokesman for Campbell's, John Faulkner, told *The New York Times* that the company was "pleased" with the consumer reaction to the initial ads, but we have our doubts about the long-term results. When the competition responds with its own negative ads, neither company is likely to be all that happy with the final results.

Even when there is no such retaliation, cheap-shot advocacy is a dangerous policy. A recent report by Mullen, a Wenham, Massachusetts, ad agency, found that consumers "are tired of feeling downbeat" and "want brands that make them feel good." Negative marketing is not calculated to meet that desire. And if your ad is seen by the public as taking unfair advantage of a rival's known weakness, it may alienate customers instead of attracting them.

For business leaders with the good sense to refrain from cheap shots, it's imperative that you follow Obama's example and establish clear parameters for your staff and suppliers, defining what you will and will not allow, and stating the consequences for failing to comply.

That task becomes somewhat more complicated in the universe of Web 2.0 and social media, particularly as to the consequences. More and more companies are turning to online communities as the most effective way to market and sell their products and services. One major problem: how to make sure that postings, blogs, and other user-generated content about your business are free of cheap shots. With that in mind, your customer-volunteers are independent operators, after all, not employees. In a community discussion of the latest developments at your company, for example, how are you going to stave off endless gossip? How do you keep questionable remarks or claims off the videos that community members are putting together?

The solution: In each community's terms of service, set forth your rules with examples of the kind of language and innuendo you will not tolerate. In your communications with members, include occasional reminders of those rules, and lay down a list of consequences for those who insist on going too far. For example, start with an informal warning, followed by temporary suspension of membership, and ending with outright banishment from the community. But having set the rules, a word of warning: Don't be too heavy-handed in enforcing them. If there's no sense of mischief and play in your social networking, the members will soon go elsewhere.

Another key problem: how to respond when your company is the target of negative consumer feedback online? The good old days when customers expressed their upset by mail or telephone are gone; now, their complaints on Facebook, MySpace, or the like are out there for all the world to read. What's worse, such postings often inspire other users to add their comments, too often echoing the first, so that, before you know it, a firestorm of criticism is raging across the Internet.

We urge you to head it off by responding to online complaints quickly, succinctly, and politely. Too often, companies delay, hoping the problem will simply go away. Too often, it just gets worse.

Some time ago, a blogger informed his 100,000 readers that he had purchased an LCD screen from Best Buy. When it broke down, he wrote, Best Buy refused to return his money. Instead of reacting quickly with an explanation of its policy, the company sat on its hands until the volume of criticism forced it to respond. Meanwhile, the damage had been spread far and wide.

When comedian Ze Frank had to stay in a hotel room with a stranger after Delta Airlines canceled his flight, he wanted some money back—and the airline refused. Frank went ballistic on his daily blog, "the show," with a funny, bawdy video that heaped blame on Delta. By the time the airline responded, the video had gone viral. Nor was Frank finished. He added a link entitled "good goes around." It took you to a page on delta.com with the headline, "chapter 11 FAQs," and the explanation, "below are answers to some of the most frequently asked questions about our chapter 11 filing."

Companies should respond to online attacks with the truth. If the complainant was in the wrong, say so clearly but without any hint of righteousness. If your company was in the wrong, admit it, promise to do better—and do so. In no event should you get into a back-and-forth, tit-for-tat exchange. State your case and leave it to the good sense of your listeners to sort out the facts. They can recognize a complainant's unreasonable argument and they will disregard it.

Like any political candidate, from Obama to the local dogcatcher, you and your company cannot afford to be seen as using unfair tactics, online or off. Voters and customers are the same people, and they have shown their distaste for cheap shots—at the cash register as well as the ballot box.

Be social: Turn CRM into CMR— the lessons of Obama Girl.

During the campaign, Barack Obama's own Web operations and his pages on social-networking sites produced an avalanche of information about the millions of volunteers flocking to his cause. The problem: How to organize all that material into a central database to be used to stay in touch with all of them. The solution: CRM, or customer relationship management software. In terms of what he had to say to his online admirers, though, and how he said it, Obama was a true believer in CMR, a customer-managed relationship.

On his Web sites, volunteers were given the tools they needed to contact voters, but it was the volunteers who decided when, where, and how the contacts would be made. In fact, in every interaction with the online masses, Obama's aides sought to build a relationship in which the masses were in charge.

One of the distinguishing characteristics of the 2008 election was the amazing proliferation of videos. Obama's team put them out there on the Web sites, and then the community took over. They decided whether to watch a film, and whether to paste it onto their blogs or MySpace pages and spread it around the globe. Using Photoshop and other tools, they created their own versions of the videos—reworking images, changing text, combining elements of different videos into so-called mashups. Some of the altered films were elaborate parodies, some were simple sight gags—like one that compared Obama to Star Trek's Mr. Spock and McCain to Batman's nemesis, the Penguin. Perhaps the best known was the video by actress and model Amber Lee Ettinger, or Obama Girl. Visitors to YouTube watched Obama Girl's suggestive performance of the "I Got a Crush … on Obama" video and its variations more than 60 million times.

Was Obama happy with all this fiddling? Not likely.
But it was happening on public space, not his
Web site, and he understood the first principle of
marketing to the social-networking world: If you
want them to do a job for you, you have to accept
that they are in charge. You're operating in their
space and they decide, from moment to moment,
whether you're going to succeed or fail in your
mission. To maximize the chances of a positive
result, Obama sought to build a strong, ongoing
relationship with the online communities. After he
earned their trust, they were more likely to welcome
him and his message.

The 200-year-old candy maker Cadbury Schweppes
knows something about the power of online
communities. With their help, Cadbury recovered
from a near-fatal string of blunders a few years back.
The remedy was a quirky campaign for its mainstay
brand, Dairy Milk chocolate—a riveting ad, nothing
remotely like what viewers might have expected
from a stodgy old company sporting the royal seal of
approval.

The 90-second clip created by Cadbury's in-house
Web wizards (A Glass and a Half Full Productions)
started in dead silence as milk was seen, but not
heard, splashing down behind the logo. Then came
eerily menacing music—the opening bars of *In the*

Air Tonight, the 1981 hit by rocker Phil Collins. "I can feel it coming in the air tonight, oh Lord," Collins crooned. Suddenly, the audience saw a gorilla's face close up, filling the screen. Eyes closed, head swaying, the creature was totally into the moment. The camera retreated, and viewers saw the big guy sitting at a trap drum set. He flexed his mighty neck muscles, sucked in deep breaths, and bam! The gorilla threw his head back, whipped his sticks in the air, and started banging in sync as the soundtrack exploded with the song's trademark drum solo. The ad closed with a shot of a Dairy Milk bar along with the Cadbury slogan: "A glass and a half full of joy." There was no voiceover, and the word chocolate never appeared.

The choice of the Collins song and a gorilla to perform it was inspired. The effect was odd, funny, weird, and totally compelling. But was this any way to sell chocolate bars? Or improve a company's public image? No, decreed a veteran Cadbury executive. Chocolate ads work only if they "make you drool," he said, and that means chocolate. Without it, "Cadbury ads lose their sensual appeal, and there go sales."

He was wrong. The gorilla ad won rave reviews from television critics when it was first shown in August 2007, and an online video version took off like a rocket in the galaxy of video-sharing sites. During its first week on YouTube, half a million people watched the gorilla perform. These volunteer marketers spread the word, and the ad quickly achieved cult status, attracting more than ten million online viewers. Then a flurry of co-creators jumped in with hundreds of user-generated takeoffs and imitations that cropped up on YouTube and other sites. Like Barack Obama, Cadbury and Collins accepted the spoofs and mashups as all part of the buzz—until, that is, Wonderbra pushed its way into the act. The ad featuring a young and nubile female model whose bust captured all the attention led Collins to charge copyright infringement. The Wonderbra version was pulled off the air.

At year's end, the original spot was named by TellyAds.com as Britain's most popular commercial of 2007. And within months, sales of Dairy Milk chocolates rose nine percent, no small number for a brand that brings in $673 million a year. What's more, Cadbury's public approval rating jumped by 20 percent, its fortunes revived by a single crowd-focused television commercial featuring a sweaty actor encased in a gorilla suit.

When all is said and done, the mountains of material you organize using CRM software will be invaluable to your organization. And your brand is likely to benefit just as much if not more from the relationships you nurture, putting the masses in charge, as it gains from any ad campaign.

BE SOCIAL: MAKE YOUR MARKETING MOBILE—THE LESSONS OF OBAMA'S CELL-PHONE STRATEGY.

Irony of ironies, the man who lived by his BlackBerry, the masterful campaigner whose savvy cell-phone strategy helped beam him to the White House, may soon be out of the loop. As president, Barack Obama will not be allowed to use a BlackBerry or cell phone.

For one thing, there's the chance that his messages might be intercepted, which could raise security issues. And the Presidential Records Act requires that all of a president's correspondence be held for examination by future generations. Still, it will be frustrating for Obama, who relied heavily on BlackBerry e-mail and text messaging to stay in touch with friends and family, particularly when separated from them for long stretches by the demands of his campaign. It also provided him with an independent flow of information from many sources. "I can imagine he will miss that freedom," one of his friends told *The New York Times.*

Obama began using wholesale text messaging in
the primaries. The technique had been used in the
2006 elections, to good effect. A study credited it
with increasing turnout among young people by
four percent. The cost per vote was $1.56, a bargain
compared to the $10 or $20 a vote for traditional
approaches such as in-person canvassing and
phone banks. On New Hampshire's primary day, his
campaign sent out three text messages to supporters,
urging them to persuade their friends and family to
vote. His margin of victory among voters 18 to 24 was
an unprecedented 40 points. A typical text message
in an early-voting state: "Register 2 vote. 2 wks left n
it takes 5 min."

At public campaign events, long before the candidate
showed up, aides would appeal to the crowd to get
on their cell phones and smart phones and call or
text message everyone they knew to come on over.
Obama supporters received a steady flow of text
and voicemail from the campaign, ranging from
press releases to word of local campaign events. The
biggest text message promotion of the campaign
was Obama's offer to tell people who shared their
cell phone number about his vice-presidential
choice before he informed the media. That added
substantially to the ever-growing list of cell-phone
contacts the campaign had been collecting from the
start, using such lures as free bumper stickers and
ring tones.

Those numbers were precious to Obama. They could be called or messaged when the campaign was rounding up volunteer workers or seeking donations; they could be contacted to remind people to register and to vote on election day. And the numbers were Obama's direct link to supporters and potential supporters, his means of maintaining a personal dialogue with thousands of them.

For volunteers like Boston's Alice Jelin Isenberg, the Obama campaign's commitment to the cell phone became evident when they showed up for a get-out-the-vote phone event. "They had a huge telephone organization going on in Boston," Isenberg told us. "They took the whole floor of a vacant building, but there were no land-line phones. When you walked in, they gave you a list of numbers to call, but you used your own cell phone. I did a lot of calling to North Carolina."

It did not escape her notice that the arrangement saved the campaign the major expense of having to install banks of phones.

A unique Obama contribution to the technology of politics was the application his team provided for the iPhone. In addition to the "Obama 08" application, it transformed the phone into a campaign instrument with separate buttons to let you learn about local

Obama events (shown in order of their proximity) and the candidate's position on issues, as well as check out campaign photos and videos.

The new telephonic social media should have a special attraction for company marketers—they separate the wheat from the chaff. To receive or send messages via cell phone or smart phone, consumers have to share their e-mail address or phone number. In effect, they're opting in to some level of relationship with the company. It's the difference between making a cold call and a call on someone who is expecting you. It means the marketers can spend their time and energy building that relationship instead of chasing their own tail.

The contest between Barack Obama and his opponents pivoted on which team could reach the most voters with the most persuasive message. That's electoral politics, replayed ever since the first Stone Age contender used cave drawings. Note carefully that even a superb message goes nowhere without a superb medium. In the end, however, Obama's familiarity with the most advanced Internet technology provided a huge advantage over opponents whose Internetspeak was always at least one technological generation behind his. Young, media-savvy Americans were completely at home with his young, media-savvy operatives.

Business leaders should take that message to heart. Only by tapping into the social technologies that Obama used so well can they hope to thrive. The lessons spelled out in this chapter can help them analyze the situation and adjust their own companies to take advantage of social networking. But the Obama campaign has yet another major lesson for us: Neither keeping your cool nor using social technologies will keep you afloat if you can't meet the final test: You must embody the change your customers want. That's the subject of the next chapter.

LESSONS

- ▶ Cultivate the new grassroots, the netroots.

- ▶ Create a seamless community.

- ▶ Nurture your lists.

- ▶ Let your netroots grow into every crevice.

- ▶ Arm yourself against, and don't take, cheap shots.

- ▶ Turn CRM into CMR.

- ▶ Make your marketing mobile.

IMPERMANENCE
RULES THE UNIVERSE.

THOSE WHO
RESIST CHANGE
RESIST REALITY
AND LIFE ITSELF.

CHAPTER 4
BE THE CHANGE

In part, Barack Obama's driving theme of change in the election of 2008 was a tactical gambit—a recognition that voters had run out of patience with two wars, a sagging economy, and the partisan bickering of conventional politics. But the change he offered went deeper than a mere ploy.

As so often promised by candidates, change is a tired cliché, six dead letters. Obama's triumph was to persuade the voters that he could bring a whole new kind of politics and government. He was appealing to the universal human yearning for growth, improvement, and a better future. And while his success was due largely to his cool, presidential persona and his mastery of social technologies, he could not have been elected without one crucial perception: He came to embody the change he promised. And the people believed that, with him, change could become reality.

Obama's change-driven election reminds us that the status quo is a dangerous place, one that business leaders should avoid at all costs, especially now. The truth is that, as the opening of this chapter notes, impermanence rules the universe. Those who resist change resist reality and life itself. They inevitably collide with contradictions that may well destroy them.

"WE ARE THE CHANGE THAT WE SEEK."—BARACK OBAMA

Change, by contrast, poses opportunities ensuring the constant rebirth that makes life viable and business exciting. Change is the engine of both politics and business, the power of growth and progress. Leaders can't afford to stand still, can't insist the present is hunky-dory. They have to sink or swim, welcoming what economist Joseph Schumpeter famously called "creative destruction."

If our business leaders don't pursue creative destruction, our economy will not recover, our industries will not regenerate, and our country will slide into depression, harming our children and grandchildren as well as ourselves. Yet if we accept the need to bury the dead and welcome the new, the worst can also trigger the best. Already, recovery ideas abound, such as new tax incentives and stimulus programs to boost marketable skills, prompt reinvestment, replace crumbling roads and bridges, create energy-efficient buildings, and get millions engaged in some of the most fundamental reengineering of America since the 1930s. If you have not yet accepted the need for drastic action, others will gladly take your place. But if you've read this far, the chances are that you're one of us—optimists eager to act fast and jump-start our country right now.

Here's how Barack Obama embraced and embodied change—and how you can, too.

BE THE CHANGE: CONFRONT REALITY AND PUT PROBLEMS IN CONTEXT—THE LESSONS OF JEREMIAH WRIGHT AND THE RACE SPEECH.

In hindsight, Barack Obama's presidential campaign came closest to collapsing in the crisis posed by the toxic sermons of his former pastor, the Rev. Jeremiah Wright Jr. But the unflinching way Obama disarmed the Wright bomb, confronting the ancient problem of race in America and reframing it in newly realistic terms, not only revitalized his candidacy but also established him as an agent of change.

In mid-March 2008, at an already uncertain moment in the primary campaign, anti-Obama agents carpeted the nation's TV screens with stunning clips of Wright denouncing the U.S. government for murdering innocent Japanese with nuclear bombs, inciting the 9/11 attacks with its own "terrorism," and persecuting African Americans with draconian drug laws while expecting them to sing *God Bless America*. Instead, Wright thundered, "God damn America for treating our citizens as less than human." Night after night, millions of Americans were shown close-ups of Wright endlessly screaming those three words, "God damn America!" on their TV sets.

Wright was widely seen as a fanatic on race to whom Obama was embarrassingly close. For nearly 20 years, he had served as Obama's pastor at Trinity United Church of Christ on Chicago's South Side. Wright had tutored Obama in Christianity and community organizing, married Obama and his wife Michelle, baptized their two daughters, and inspired the title of Obama's second book, *The Audacity of Hope.*

Obama's top advisers were aghast at the potential effect on racially combustible white voters. They also feared that the issue would so discourage African Americans about Obama's chances that it would leave them enraged and possibly defeatist. David Axelrod's instinct was to cut Wright dead, ignore the race issue, and hope for the best. Obama himself acknowledged that moving on without comment was probably the "politically safe" course.

But Barack Obama is a realist. He was convinced that a leader could not avoid a serious challenge to something so central to his being. He understood that he had to respond or risk losing both respect and authenticity.

But how? He might have simply limited himself to talking about his past relationship with Wright and, as he had before, disavowing Wright's extremism. Instead, he chose to confront the issue behind the issue. As America's first viable black presidential candidate, he decided, he could not, should not pretend that his race was not the elephant in the room. He would bet the bank on his belief that Americans' attitudes had changed, that they were ready to judge their potential leaders on the basis of intelligence, experience, and philosophy rather than racial identity.

Obama had just undergone a three-hour grilling by the *Chicago Tribune*, which demanded every detail of his past relationship with a Chicago fixer named Tony Rezko. Though exhausted, Obama told Axelrod, "I want to do a speech on race." He knew the speech could doom his candidacy: "Either they will accept it or they won't, and I won't be President." But if he lost, he said, "I will have done something valuable."

For the next three nights, his nervous advisers stayed out of his way while he wrote the speech, an answer to Wright's rants that brilliantly elevated the subject from an embarrassment to a personal triumph.

Delivered in Philadelphia at a museum devoted
to the U.S. Constitution, the address was a half-
hour tour de force that echoed the Constitution's
historic goal of forming "a more perfect union." As
Newsweek reported, Obama recalled his mother's
advice to look for the good in people and empathize
with their hopes and fears. He acknowledged racial
progress in the United States, but he also described
in unblinking detail the reality of residual tensions
between millions of blacks and whites. Showing not a
trace of either anger or fear, he empathized both with
the anger of blacks at their treatment and with his
white grandmother's fear of black men on the street.

Stuck in "a racial stalemate," Obama said, the
country has a choice. "We can play Reverend Wright's
sermons on every channel, every day, and talk about
them from now until the election.... We can pounce
on some gaffe by a Hillary supporter as evidence
that she's playing the race card, or we can speculate
on whether white men will all flock to John McCain.
We can do that. But if we do, I can tell you that in
the next election, we'll be talking about some other
distraction. And then another one. And then another
one. And then nothing will change."

Obama offered a different choice: Vote for him and
seize the opportunity for blacks and whites to join
together in solving the country's problems, from

health care to failing schools to interminable wars. He transformed the Wright issue from a divider to a uniter. He used it as the occasion for bringing racism out of the campaign closet and calling upon Americans as one people of many colors to strive for "a more perfect union."

Obama's speech brought many, both black and white, to tears. It was widely praised; in some quarters, it was viewed as a major turning point in his campaign. His faith in the nation's ability to change had been confirmed. And not incidentally, he had shown the race issue in a realistic light that the nation could accept. He had become the change that he was offering.

Though the specific issues will, of course, be very different, Obama's decision to confront the issue set a memorable example for any business leader confronted with a serious challenge to his or her company's well-being. On one level, Obama demonstrated that there is no gain to be had by putting your head in the sand and pretending the problem doesn't exist. It is far better to stand up and confront your attacker with the truth.

THOSE WHO RESIST CHANGE RESIST REALITY.

On another level, Obama's decision holds a lesson
for companies that resist any challenge to the status
quo. Business has, in recent years, produced a
plethora of fugitives from reality, the leaders of such
troubled organizations as AIG, Citigroup, ImClone,
Lehman Brothers, Tyco, and United Way. Typically,
these people recoil from the consequences of
their follies as if they had been absent when things
somehow went sour. In extreme cases, as at AIG
after the 2008 bailout, they party on using taxpayers'
money; with $85 billion in federal cash stuffing its
pockets, AIG promptly flew its top executives to a
posh California spa for a weekend of fun costing
$443,000.

Most businesspeople, however, see danger signals
long before disaster strikes—and even so, they make
no changes or merely temporize. It boils down to
this: If you see a major change on the horizon, ask
whether it represents a better way of doing business.
And if the answer is yes, don't just walk—run to
embrace it.

We understand that it's not all that simple. By
their very nature, organizations—especially large
ones—resist change. It threatens perks built up over
decades; it threatens jobs. But many companies have
suffered because they refused to adjust to a new

business reality. In point of fact, winning companies don't just embrace change—they lead the way. They are the change.

BE THE CHANGE: WHEN YOU'RE ON SOLID GROUND, DON'T BACK OFF—THE LESSONS OF CLASHING WITH HILLARY CLINTON ON FOREIGN POLICY.

At a pivotal moment early in Barack Obama's presidential run, the candidate showed his backbone in a way that delighted his staff and helped to define his campaign. Rather than taking the time-honored Washington route of softening or shying away from a stated position to prevent a competitor from gaining ground—fairly or unfairly—Obama chose a new path: He embraced change by standing behind his original statement. And he did it because he knew he was right the first time.

The incident occurred in July 2007, in a debate among the eight Democratic candidates sponsored by CNN and YouTube. Obama was asked if he would be willing to meet, without preconditions, with the leaders of Cuba, Iran, North Korea, Syria, and Venezuela to reduce the tensions dividing the world. His unhesitating answer: "I would."

Like a fox on a field mouse, Hillary Clinton pounced.
"I don't want to be used for propaganda purposes,"
she said. Obama was naïve, she implied, showing his
lack of experience and diplomatic know-how. "I will
use a lot of high-level presidential envoys to test
the waters, to feel the way," she said, but a sensible
president would never "promise a meeting at that
high a level before you know what the intentions
are." It was a forceful and effective attack.

Obama's staffers knew immediately that this would
be headline fodder and that Clinton's people would
assault his position relentlessly. In a conference call
the next morning, key aides were debating how to
respond. "We have the sense they're going to come
after us on it," recalled communications director Dan
Pfeiffer. "And we're all on the bus trying to figure out
how to get out of it, how not to talk about it."

Obama had been listening to the conversation, and
now he broke in. "This is ridiculous," one staffer
recalls him saying. "We met with Stalin. We met with
Mao. The idea that we can't meet with Ahmadinejad
is ridiculous. This is a bunch of Washington-insider
conventional wisdom that makes no sense. We
should not run from this debate. We should have it."

Like a shot of adrenaline, his response galvanized
the troops. With no more talk of evading the issue,

they put out a memo taking the offensive—and the aftermath told the young, inexperienced staffers that they could take on the Clinton machine and hold their own. They had been on tiptoe, hesitant to rouse what Pfeiffer called "the most impressive, toughest, most ruthless war room in the world." Now, "It was like we had taken our first punch and kept on going."

Holding the solid ground is a lesson that many business leaders need to learn. Too often, a company caught in the glare of controversy will retreat in confusion, conceding far too much in the panicky hope of escaping "bad publicity." To be sure, when you are actually in the wrong, the best thing to do is to admit it and make amends. But when you can make a solid case that you are doing the right thing—or even that you have chosen the lesser evil—it's far better to offer a reasoned explanation than to back off.

A case of product tampering at Pepsi provides a strong lesson in dealing with hoaxes or any other unjustified public attack. Some 15 years ago, a man in Tacoma, Washington, claimed that he had popped the top on a can of Diet Pepsi only to find a syringe floating in the liquid inside. A string of copycat claims followed, most of which were quickly disproved and the perpetrators apprehended. But Pepsi's leaders didn't flinch. Instead, knowing that the claims were false, they wasted no time in addressing the situation and kept up their offensive even as the accusers were discredited.

That quick reaction stemmed from their well-defined sense of priorities: Their first concern was the purity of their product and the safety of their customers, a principle that allowed them to swing into action without having to discuss what their response should be. Similarly, Barack Obama knew that his position was the correct one, and he wasted no time in hedging his bets or second-guessing his response. Instead, he told his staff to take the offensive against the Clinton machine.

Communication with employees, the press, and customers was critical to Pepsi's crisis management. The company's leaders had learned of the tampering problem soon after the claim was made when their Seattle franchise bottler was contacted by a local television station. Pepsi's leaders quickly alerted their stakeholders—the president updated employees every morning during the crisis week, and customers and bottlers were kept informed through an 800-number help line. People in the field talked to customers at retail outlets.

Staying close to all these stakeholders, separating fact from fiction, and holding onto loyal customers helped Pepsi weather the crisis. The corporation did lose millions of dollars in sales until the storm subsided, but fate smiled on the soft-drink maker with particularly hot summer weather that sent sales soaring just a few weeks later.

CHANGE IS THE ENGINE OF BUSINESS, THE POWER OF GROWTH AND PROGRESS.

Every organization has to confront a crisis sooner or later, and the blueprint Pepsi laid out after its harrowing week is worth remembering:

- ▶ Clearly define lines of authority.

- ▶ Contact stakeholders in appropriate order.

- ▶ Designate a primary point person and a backup at each company location.

- ▶ Make decisions based on facts, not hearsay.

- ▶ Take disciplinary action, if called for, through proper channels.

- ▶ Continue normal day-to-day operations.

Be the change: Never forget the power of the personal touch—the lesson of Obama's thank-you call.

Sometimes the change a leader embraces can seem small and inconsequential, when, in reality, it springs from a much larger change in his organization's way of operating.

Boston business consultant Alice Jelin Isenberg has long been a fixture in Democratic presidential campaigns. In the 2008 election season, she volunteered to work on Barack Obama's New England Steering Committee. What the committee members wanted to steer was money into the campaign's coffers.

Isenberg has every reason to be proud of her efforts, but her most memorable moment had nothing to do with a generous donor signing a hefty check. Rather, it was the night in December 2007 when she picked up her phone to hear: "Hello, Alice? This is Barack Obama." Isenberg was so startled that she momentarily thought of replying, "Yes, and I'm the Queen of England." But there was something recognizable about the voice.

A couple of nights previously, Isenberg had introduced Obama to between 300 and 400 people at a Fenway Park fundraiser. Facing a crowd that big typically makes her nervous, she told us, but on that night, Obama's friendliness put her at ease. "And I did a great job—at least, that's what my husband says, and he's pretty critical," she grinned.

Apparently, Barack Obama agreed with Isenberg's husband. The candidate was calling to thank her for her "lovely introduction" at Fenway Park. In her many years of working behind the scenes for political candidates, Isenberg says she never before got a phone call like this.

Barack Obama was committed from the beginning to making this a new kind of campaign, and he has succeeded in changing the status quo of politics in ways that may seem small, but, upon closer examination, turn out to be larger than they first appeared. Thanking volunteers is very much a part of that, and Obama makes a point at his rallies of showing gratitude to them along with hailing local dignitaries. As Isenberg is quick to point out, it takes an "incredible organization, an enormous amount of staff work" to pull off calls to everyone who has introduced Obama at some event. "I can't tell you how much it meant to me."

Mike Abrashoff, a naval captain turned author and speaker, knows the importance of saying "thank you." In his first book, *It's Your Ship*, he related how he sent letters to the parents of his crew members on the guided-missile destroyer USS *Benfold*. Putting himself in those parents' shoes, he imagined how happy they would be to hear from the commanding officer that their sons and daughters were doing well. And he figured that those parents would, in turn, call their children to tell them how proud they were of them.

Abrashoff debated whether to send a letter to the parents of one young man who wasn't really star material. Weighing the sailor's progress, he decided to go ahead. A couple of weeks later, the sailor appeared at his door, tears streaming down his face. It seems that the kid's father had always considered him a failure and told him so. After reading the captain's letter, he called to congratulate his son and tell him how proud he was of him. "Captain, I can't thank you enough," said the young man. For the first time in his life, he felt loved and encouraged by his father.

As Abrashoff says, "Leadership is the art of practicing simple things—commonsense gestures that ensure high morale and vastly increase the odds of winning." In other words, small changes can have big consequences.

Be the change: Get unfiltered information—the lessons of Obama's internal communication strategy.

Yes-men and women may be a delight to the ear of a harried leader, but listening to them typically leads to disaster in the long run. For the best results, leaders need to make sure their people are truly comfortable sharing ideas and feelings. Whether it's a member of a ship's crew, an engineer, or a production-line worker, the person giving information or an opinion has to be confident that, no matter what, expressing a viewpoint will not draw a penalty. If that sort of atmosphere is lacking in your company, our best advice is to embrace and embody change yesterday, if not sooner. The goal is to get your employees to tell you how they would improve your company's operations, and the less constrained they feel, the more you're going to learn and the more your organization will benefit.

A stickler for keeping confidential campaign information confidential, Barack Obama made it safe and comfortable for his inner circle to share their ideas, concerns, and heartfelt beliefs. They knew that what they said wouldn't be leaked to a gotcha reporter or used to advantage by a rival campaign's staff. Internal strife, if there was any, was kept under wraps. No one in the Obama inner circle was publicly berated for mistakes.

Uninhibited ideas are also at the heart of the creative process. At HTC, the Taiwan-based mobile phone manufacturer, no-holds-barred conversations are routine in a unit called Magic Labs, the company's innovation center. Its 60 so-called magicians represent a universe of talent, from electrical and mechanical engineers to graphic designers and software writers. Their mission is to come up with ideas very fast and very cheaply. Most of the ideas are worthless, but, as *Fast Company* magazine pointed out recently, HTC's leaders don't criticize or penalize the originators. Rather, they applaud the effort. That's the way the HTC innovation process is supposed to work.

IF YOU SEE A MAJOR CHANGE ON THE HORIZON, IF YOU ARE CONFIDENT THAT IT REPRESENTS A BETTER WAY OF DOING BUSINESS, DON'T JUST WALK—RUN TO EMBRACE IT.

In fact, Magic Labs is "designed to fail," says John Wang, HTC's chief marketing officer (aka chief innovation wizard). The unit, which Wang founded, is organized around brainstorming sessions at which members offer up hundreds of ideas for new products or improvements on old ones, all within the space of about an hour. Many such sessions take place over the course of a day, with participants spewing out ideas and viewing prototypes of promising concepts from previous sessions. The prototypes very quickly prove or disprove the viability of an intriguing idea. As Wang explains, what seems like a great idea can fall apart quickly when you touch the prototype and see how it works.

Almost everything that comes out of a brainstorming session is doomed—and that's just as it should be: HTC isn't interested in wasting money on bad ideas. It may take 1,000 ideas to find one or two that are true business winners like the recently introduced HTC Dream, Google's answer to the Apple iPhone. But from the HTC leadership's point of view, the cost of discarding 999 ideas is minimal compared to the value produced by the few that work. Magic Labs is set up to fail efficiently.

What fascinates us is the way the brainstorming sessions are conducted. To make sure members are engaged in original thinking, Magic Labs resorts to what it calls "zero learning." The ideators put aside what they've learned about the subject under discussion and attempt to revert to babyhood, reacting to a problem on an intuitive level. The idea is to think like a baby who hasn't learned much yet.

In designing phones, the watchwords at HTC are simplicity and usability, attributes that have been lost in the glut of features added to mobile phones in recent years. Magic Labs wanted to find a way to make the phones more user-friendly, but it was getting nowhere. Taking a page from the baby book, the brainstormers had to forget about the mechanical details and think about how children intuitively interact with an object. They don't want to read manuals or even push buttons up and down. Their instinct is to reach out and touch the object. From that insight came the HTC Dream with its 3-D cube that you turn with your finger to move between programs.

HTC leaders give each idea, no matter how wacky, a thorough and respectful hearing. As a result, the company has emerged as one of the world's leading manufacturers of mobile phones.

Though we have been focusing on how you should listen to your employees, other people in your business life deserve your attention, too. Your customers, for example. For Barack Obama, his customers are the American people, both those who elected him and those whose votes went elsewhere. During the campaign, he used his Web site to solicit his customers' opinions—and he plans on keeping that line and others open even after he takes up residence in the White House.

Anne Sellers's advice to "listen first, talk second," works well for companies as well as candidates. She is the managing principal and majority owner of Sensory Technologies, a $20 million company based in Indianapolis, Indiana, that provides all sorts of audiovisual services—from videoconferencing system design to Web streaming and distribution. When profiled in *Smart Business Indianapolis*, Sellers said frontline employees are "the people who deal with the grit of your business, see the trends, sense the mood of your clients, know whether money is being made or lost. You have to trust them." It's only after you know what they consider to be important, and what's getting in the way of them doing their jobs, that you can take action to fix the problems.

Sellers says she does her best listening while visiting clients and employees just as a major project is winding down. "First, you get to spend time with the clients and hear firsthand their degree of satisfaction," she explains. "But more importantly, the employees get to show off their work, and you get to be proud of that employee. Then you get to hear how it went, what the challenges are, how to make things better, what needs your attention in the future."

"LISTEN FIRST, TALK SECOND."

Anne Sellers is a good example of a leader who understands that there is no substitute for getting out of the corner office and listening to employees in the field and the customers they serve. Larry Bossidy, the now retired but still legendary Honeywell CEO, is another. As Bossidy once reminded, "Don't make the mistake of thinking you can lead with your feet up on the desk."

As president, Barack Obama is bound to find himself isolated from the straight talk he coveted during the campaign. It remains to be seen whether President Obama will be able to continue providing protection for truth tellers given the notoriously leaky Capitol Hill apparatus. The steady drip of unauthorized information during his cabinet-selection process doesn't bode well for the future. It's one thing for a small group of campaign aides to keep confidential information from spreading. But even the most leak-proof campaign operation would be challenged by the infusion of enormous numbers of congressional staffers privy to critical information but without the degree of loyalty Obama has come to expect from his closest advisers.

Nevertheless, we can still hold out hope that, with his instinct for and commitment to change, President Obama will find a way to plug the leaks and reform a Washington culture that puts the leader of the free world at a disadvantage when it comes to accessing unfiltered information.

BE THE CHANGE: SHARE YOUR VISION OF THE FUTURE—THE LESSONS OF OBAMA'S LETTERS TO FEDERAL EMPLOYEES.

Just weeks before the election, Barack Obama wrote a remarkable set of letters to employees at seven federal agencies. Each of the letters was tailored to meet the concerns of a particular agency, and each of them communicated his vision of the future in a manner calculated to inspire and energize its recipients on his behalf.

In the letters, the candidate tapped into a widespread discontent, offering strong critiques of the Bush administration. Beyond that, he described his position on dozens of issues in greater detail than

he ever had on the campaign trail and laid out a
blueprint of where he wanted to take the government
and the country.

John Gage, president of the 600,000-member
American Federation of Government Employees,
had suggested that Obama write the letters, and the
union distributed them. "I asked him to put it in
writing, something I could use with my members,"
Gage told *The Washington Post,* "and he didn't flinch.
The fact that he's willing to put his name to it is a
good sign."

The letter to the Labor Department employees,
for example, charged that Bush appointees had
frustrated efforts to keep workers safe, especially
miners, a major mission of the agency. "Our mine
safety program will have the staffing ... needed to get
the job done," Obama promised. He also presented
a list of programs he wanted the department to bird-
dog: "I believe that it's time we stopped talking about
family values and start pursuing policies that truly
value families, such as paid family leave, flexible
work schedules, and telework, with the federal
government leading by example."

In his letters to employees at the Department of
Housing and Urban Development, Obama promised
to halt the Bush administration's moves to cut the

agency's payroll while farming out some of its tasks to outside contractors. He also wrote that "HUD must be part of the solution" to the housing crisis, offering the prospect of an important new role for an agency that has been marginalized in recent years.

By all accounts, the letters struck a chord with their recipients, inspiring many to support Obama and work for his election. By speaking directly to the particular issues of the various departments, and sharing his goals for the future, he moved the employees to act on his behalf.

That same approach led more than a million people from all walks of life to join the Obama campaign as volunteers. We talked with one of them, 63-year-old Dorothy Terrell, of Boston, Massachusetts. She is currently a Venture Partner at First Light Capital and previously held positions at Digital Equipment Corporation, Sun Microsystems (as president of SunExpress, an operating company), and NMS Communications. She serves on the board of General Mills, Herman Miller, and Endeca Technologies. She had been deeply disturbed by the policies of the Bush administration, and as the primary season dawned, she feared "what I saw coming down the pike."

Obama's ideas and agenda addressed those fears, and Terrell signed on for the duration. She joined his

New England Steering Committee at its inception in
February 2007, and for almost 22 months she lived
his campaign.

"For the folks I know and those I met along the way,"
she recalls, "these were desperate times, and they
called for desperate measures. I guess falling in line
is a desperate measure for a traditionally unruly
group of people."

Terrell went to South Carolina during the primary
season, where she spent days calling people already
identified as Obama voters to make sure they knew
where the polls were and reminding them to vote.
She also went to San Antonio to help a friend form a
Texas Women for Obama group. In Virginia, during
the general election, she helped "clean the lists"—
winnow out the voters who would definitely not vote
for Obama. That saved the campaign from wasting
huge amounts of time and money.

Everywhere she went, Terrell says, there were
masses of volunteers, local and out-of-state (even
international), skilled and unskilled, all of them
"ready to do what it took to make it happen." In
Richmond, a man in a wheelchair rolled in: "He
couldn't see very well, and he couldn't use the phone
system, which went back to dial tone if you didn't
dial quickly enough. There was no fanfare. They

found him a magnifying glass and a phone he could control and he went to work. It was just like he walked in on two legs, no big deal. I really felt proud."

Wherever she went, Terrell wore an Obama pin and/ or bracelet. "I got a lot of people talking that way," she says. That's what happened at a business lunch with a woman in New York. When the woman saw the pin, she said she was eternally grateful to Obama because he and his message had inspired her college-age son, who was "never interested in anything," to become actively committed to the campaign. The woman gave Terrell a check for $2,300.

"I got money from people I barely knew," Terrell recalls, "and they all had stories about not ever writing a check for a political campaign before but that this time they felt so differently."

We asked Terrell about the high point of her experience—was it election night? "It probably was," she replied, "but I was numb. I had worked the polls as an Obama observer from 6:30 in the morning until 8 o'clock. No parties for me—I went straight home and flopped. I suppose the real high for me was the work and the people. There were so many kindred souls." And in the end, what stuck with her was that so many different kinds of people—different in terms of age, gender, race, and class—had joined hands in response to Obama's message.

A message that unites people, that speaks to their larger hopes and gives them and their work a greater sense of importance, is a powerful motivator. Fred Smith, the man who founded a parcel delivery service and built it into the global giant FedEx, has delivered that message all through the years.

"I don't want my employees thinking about the minimum amount of effort they have to put in to keep from getting fired," he told *Fortune* magazine. "I want them thinking about the best possible job they could do if everybody was giving 100 percent of their effort." His key for getting that effort: Persuade employees that their jobs have meaning and purpose. "We still tell our employees what we always told them," Smith said: "'You're delivering the most important commerce in the history of the world. You're not delivering sand and gravel. You're delivering someone's pacemaker, chemotherapy treatment for cancer drugs, the part that keeps the F-18s flying, or the legal brief that decides the case.'"

That's a lesson businesspeople too often neglect. All of us, and that includes your employees, need to hear messages that confirm our self-worth and give us the impetus to strive to do better. The communication of those messages, the sharing of the company's vision of the present and future, should be high on the agenda of every business leader.

BE THE CHANGE: FORGET THE SQUABBLES, STRENGTHEN THE TEAM—THE LESSONS OF THE TRANSITION.

The greatest leaders—whether in business, politics, or the military—are willing to share power and prestige to get the results their enterprise most needs. George Marshall knew he wasn't the right man to command the European front and recommended Dwight Eisenhower for the job. Abraham Lincoln invited his most prestigious rivals to join his cabinet in the Civil War, knowing he needed the best men available to save the Union. Both leaders had no trouble embracing the changes their chosen associates would surely propose because they knew the country they loved so deeply would benefit from new ideas and ways of acting.

And then there is Indra Nooyi, a business leader cut from the same cloth as Marshall and Lincoln. In 2006, when she was told she had won the competition to be CEO of PepsiCo, her first move, according to *Fortune*, was to fly to Cape Cod, where her chief rival was vacationing, to plead with him not to leave the company. Most new bosses would shrug off the resignation of a challenger. Some might welcome it, or even give a nudge. But the India-born Nooyi and Mike White had been friends and rising stars at PepsiCo for years. She knew he was the company's best operations man, an important adviser, and a guy who would be indispensable in a crisis. "He could easily have been CEO," she explained; why should she do without that kind of talent?

So, on the beach at Cape Cod, she said, "Tell me whatever I need to do to keep you, and I will do it." And when White agreed to stay, she asked the board to raise his compensation nearly as high as her own $7.1 million package. At key meetings, he always sits on her right. "I treat Mike as my partner," she says. And beyond any doubt, that arrangement is what's best for PepsiCo's results—and in the end, for Indra Nooyi, too.

Barack Obama took a page from Nooyi's book by naming Hillary Clinton as his secretary of state, promising her direct access to him and allowing her to choose her own staff. It was an act of supreme self-confidence, and one that brought into the Obama administration a world-class intellect and well-known global emissary whose credentials will earn her a respectful welcome in world capitals.

Obama reached out to her to form a partnership based on mutual respect and self-interest. The rapprochement between two tough adversaries actually began at the Denver convention in August, when Clinton shrugged off the enmities of the primary campaign and gave her impassioned endorsement of the Democratic nominee and continued to campaign for him with gusto in the months leading up to Election Day on November 4, 2008.

Those two bedfellows were not quite as strange as they first appeared. Rival primary campaigns often make for a rush among candidates to put daylight between their very similar policies. As in the case of Obama and Clinton, when the battle has ended and the traditional party orbits exert their gravitational pull, the gap closes.

In any case, the importance of the vaunted personal relationships between presidents and their secretaries of state, à la George H.W. Bush and James Baker, may not be all they're cracked up to be. Just look at the George W. Bush and Condoleezza Rice track record. Their long and genuine friendship did not translate into important foreign policy achievements.

In politics as in business, putting aside personal animosities and reining in competitive instincts to do what's best for your country or your company is the kind of change that can turn your enterprise around and put it back on top.

BE THE CHANGE: SEE YOURSELF CLEARLY—THE LESSONS OF THE DEBATES.

Talk is cheap; change is dear—especially when the change most needed begins with you, the woman or man whose name appears at the top of the organizational chart.

Barack Obama has been justly praised for his oratory, for his political instincts, and for the quality of both the advisers he chose and the campaign they ran. But as a candidate, perhaps his greatest asset was his ability to assess his own performance and his strengths and weaknesses. To some of his aides, Obama's self-appraisal seemed uncanny, almost inhuman, as if he were judging someone else—and not always someone he particularly liked.

Nowhere did that talent show itself better than in Obama's preparation for his campaign debates. After an early run-in with Hillary Clinton over health care, Obama told his strategist David Axelrod that she had beaten him, and he would have to do better.

At the height of the campaign in August, however, Obama was still learning. He was especially critical of his performance against McCain in a pseudo-debate in which the evangelist Rick Warren interviewed the candidates one after the other, asking each the same set of questions. The pundits judged that McCain's brief, pithy answers beat Obama's professorial ramblings, and Obama agreed. So he prepped for the three formal debates, spread over three weeks ending in mid-October, like an NFL quarterback getting ready for the Super Bowl.

Obama memorized tirelessly, soaking up details about everything from the gross national product and the federal budget to the arcana of new weapons systems. Each fact was a bullet for shooting down the canard that he didn't know enough to be president. But Obama and his advisers knew that the overall impression he left with voters would be the key to success in the debates. Facing the veteran John McCain, with his record of personal heroism and long Senate experience, Obama had to avoid personal attacks and come off as calm, authoritative, and in control—in a word, presidential.

Through the late summer and early fall, the Democratic candidate and his team rehearsed repeatedly for the first debate, using a set in

Clearwater, Florida, that was an exact replica of
the debate site at the University of Mississippi.
The role of McCain was played by Gregory Craig,
a top-flight Washington trial lawyer who had been
among the first people to urge Obama to make the
presidential run.

A polished cross-examiner, Craig could be tough,
and he played McCain as a stern commander
condescending to the neophyte, as *Newsweek* tells
it. "Do not lecture me about the war," he growled
at Obama in one rehearsal. "Do not tell me how to
deploy men in combat. I was flying a jet over Vietnam
when you were in grade school." In response, Obama
was respectful but unintimidated; he practiced a
counterattack that began, "You were wrong about
Iraq," and went on to a litany of other McCain errors
in judgment. If McCain were to criticize Obama's
willingness to meet with the likes of Cuba's Fidel
Castro and Iran's Mahmoud Ahmadinejad, Obama
was primed to respond that McCain had even
refused to meet with the president of Spain and
had once said it would be good enough to "muddle
through" in Afghanistan.

Through it all, Barack Obama remained poised and
self-aware, comfortably inhabiting his own persona.
"I'm a little tired and a little cranky," he said at one
point. "I'm going to my room for a half-hour and I'll

be in better shape to work with." Sure enough, in 30 minutes he showed up ready to perform.

Obama's sense of irony never deserted him, particularly when he had to assume the appropriate air of dramatic indignation at one of McCain's follies. He broke up in laughter when he heard himself sternly intoning, "You wouldn't even talk to the president of Spain!" And whatever happened, he remained unrattled and a bit detached. Once, when some power anomaly set the lights to flickering like strobe fixtures in a 1970s' disco, Obama kept his position at the podium, softly singing to himself. The song was *Disco Inferno.*

TALK IS CHEAP; CHANGE IS DEAR.

In at least one rehearsal, Obama got angry at Craig's baiting. But when he watched the video, he realized he looked petulant and petty. Showing anger was counterproductive, and he told himself that there would be no shouting or interrupting McCain. His debate coach, Michael Sheehan, set the goal as making McCain look like Mr. Wilson, the cranky neighbor who was always yelling at the comic-strip urchin Dennis the Menace.

Business leaders should absorb two messages from Obama's meticulous preparation for the debates. The first and most obvious is to be ruthless in gauging your own performance, with all its virtues and flaws. Business history teems with the fiascos of men and women deluded into thinking they could carry off critical situations. We need only mention the recent congressional hearings on a bailout for the auto industry, when the heads of the Big Three automakers failed abysmally in trying to make their case.

Lesson number two that emerges from Obama's debate rehearsals is the value of preparation and practice. Training and staff-development programs are costly and time-consuming, but they pay big dividends. General Electric and Motorola, for example, built their famously deep management teams through costly staff-development programs. And new employees at The Container Store average 241 hours of training—more than six full weeks—stretched out over their first year. It seems to work: The Container Store averages sales of $400 per square foot, versus just $125 for the rest of the housewares industry. And for eight straight years, the company has topped the *Fortune* list of the 100 best companies to work for.

Practice paid off for Obama, too. He didn't win every point in his three debates with John McCain, but he was poised and unruffled. And although McCain never came off looking like "Mr. Wilson," his performance was uneven and occasionally tired. Especially in the second, "town-hall meeting" encounter, Obama sat calmly on his stool as McCain stumped around the stage, repeating the phrase "my friends" until it sounded like a verbal tic. And after the third debate, with McCain's repeated and increasingly strained invocations of "Joe the Plumber," it was clearly Obama who had come through the series as the more presidential of the two candidates.

Without the intensive rehearsals by a candidate whose relentless scrutiny of himself never flags, the outcome could well have been different. But it is not just Obama's ability to recognize the need to change his behavior that counts; it's having the self-confidence and determination to push ahead until he reaches his goal.

Way back in the Middle Ages of 2007, when Barack Obama was the odd name of a little-known Chicago politician, "change" was a campaign cliché, far removed from the heart-throbbing, torch-flaming call to arms needed to elect the next Leader of The Free World. That Obama revived the word, breathing new life into six dead letters, is one of his astonishing if less noticed accomplishments. Only a genius of sorts can turn insipid, meaningless change into actual, real-life "CHANGE!"

The beauty of Obama's transmutation is that it re-teaches the value of change as the essence of life, renewing for millions the power of welcoming a new order instead of being scared by it. Reminiscent of frontier America, that outlook is especially needed in today's tormented business world, panicked by recession and ambiguous directions to safety. The status quo is a deadly trap. Leave at once. Embrace change with a spirit of audacity, confidence, and realism. Go for it, *now*.

LESSONS

- ▶ Confront reality and put problems in context.

- ▶ When you're on solid ground, don't back off.

- ▶ Share your vision of the future.

- ▶ Forget the squabbles, strengthen the team.

- ▶ Never forget the power of the personal touch.

- ▶ Get unfiltered information.

- ▶ See yourself clearly.

THE ELECTION OF BARACK
OBAMA TO BE PRESIDENT
OF THE UNITED STATES IS
SURELY ONE OF THE LEAST
LIKELY STORIES OF OUR TIME,
AND ITS MEANINGS AND
CONSEQUENCES WILL PLAY
OUT FOR DECADES TO COME.
BUT ALL AMERICANS—AND IN
PARTICULAR, ALL BUSINESS
LEADERS—HAVE MUCH TO
LEARN FROM THE WAY OBAMA
WON HIS VICTORY, AND THESE
LESSONS ARE ALREADY CLEAR
TO ANYONE WHO WANTS TO
READ THEM.

EPILOGUE

We hope that all of our readers, along with their businesses, will profit from these lessons. And we hope that our conversation won't end with this book. In the coming months, we'll have more to say—and, we expect to learn more from you at our Web site, barackinc.com.

Not all of us are genetically blessed with the remarkably calm and rational temperament that helped Obama keep his cool and stay relentlessly on message throughout the marathon campaign. But psychologists have shown that we can train ourselves to control strong emotions, ignore irrelevant distractions, and stay focused on the issues that really matter. You can do it, too.

On the surface, it would seem easier to emulate Obama's second major strategy—his use of social technologies to create the vast national community of donors, supporters, volunteers, and full-time campaigners who carried him to victory. But many business leaders are not yet comfortable with the far reaches of the Internet, and have not yet begun to contemplate the use of the blogs, viral videos, text messages, and cell-phone networks that are essential to form a community that can nurture a business. We hope this book will introduce social technologies, begin to explain them, and encourage their use.

Obama's final strategy—to base his campaign on change—may be hardest of all to adapt to business, but it is also the most crucial. Change is eternal; change is business opportunity; change is life itself. To deal with it means accepting change not as a superficial slogan, but as a world-transforming new order and a continuing process. It requires you to confront new realities without illusion and to assess your own strengths and handicaps with an unflinching eye. And if you are to succeed, you will have to become the change that you seek—to embrace and embody change so persuasively that your people, like Obama's voters, will want to join you in changing the world.

If that seems a tall order, remember that Barack Obama won his race. And the prize is as worthwhile for you as it is for him. Just as his vision and reward can be government for all of us, you can build a business that focuses on what really matters—the entire community that it involves. Your company will be of the people, by the people, and for the people.

Let's go change the world.

"President 2.0: Obama harnessed the grass-roots power of the Web to get elected. How will he use that power now?" Daniel Lyons and Daniel Stone, *Newsweek*, December 1, 2008.

"Apple: The Genius Behind Steve," Adam Lashinsky, Michal Lev-Ram, and Mina Kimes, *Fortune*, November 24, 2008, p. 70.

"Obama's Lincoln," Evan Thomas and Richard Wolffe, *Newsweek*, November 24, 2008.

"Obama Team Anything but Shy and Retiring," Helene Cooper, *The New York Times*, November 18, 2008.

"Battle Plans, How Obama Won," Ryan Lizza, *The New Yorker (online)*, November 17, 2008.

"Center Stage," Evan Thomas, *Newsweek*, November 17, 2008.

"Going Into Battle," Evan Thomas, *Newsweek*, November 17, 2008.

SOURCES

"Hey, Mr. President-Elect, Got a Minute...Or 10?" Howard Fineman, *Newsweek*, November 17, 2008.

"How He Did It," Evan Thomas, *Newsweek*, November 17, 2008.

"Improvising to Create An Unlikely Success Story," Pete Thamel, *The New York Times*, November 17, 2008.

"Obama and the Risk of Disillusioned Fans," Peter Baker, *International Herald Tribune*, November 17, 2008.

"Obama Wrote Federal Staffers About His Goals...," Carol D. Leonnig, The Washington Post, November 17, 2008, p. A.1.

"The Age of Obama," Jon Meacham, *Newsweek*, November 17, 2008.

"The Final Days," Evan Thomas, *Newsweek*, November 17, 2008.

"The Great Debates," Evan Thomas, *Newsweek*, November 17, 2008.

"This Social Network Is Up and Running," Jay Greene, *BusinessWeek*, November 17, 2008, p. 74-76.

"Bosses checking up on workers via Facebook: Profiles full of wild party pics…," Kirsten Valle, *McClatchy-Tribune Business News*, November 16, 2008.

"Racy and negative ads found to be ineffective," *Richmond Times-Dispatch*, November 16, 2008, p. E.2.

"The Election Lives," Gail Collins, *The New York Times*, November 13, 2008, p. A.37.

"Born to Hand Jive," Josh Quittner, *Time*, Special Issue/The Choice, November 10, 2008, p. 109.

"Visa uses Facebook network to reach small businesses," Kate Maddox, *B to B*, November 10, 2008, Vol. 93, Iss. 16, p. 29.

"Inner Circle: Obama's Closely Knit Group Offered Comfort, Advice in Campaign," Peter Nicholas, *South Florida Sun–Sentinel*, November 9, 2008, p. A.1.

"The Obama story: The improbable journey," Jonathan Freedland, *The Guardian*, November 6, 2008, p. 2.

"The Vote: A Victory for Social Media, Too," Arik Hesseldahl, Douglas MacMillan, and Olga Kharif, *BusinessWeek* (online), November 6, 2008.

"Near-Flawless Run from Start to Finish Is Credited in Victory," Adam Nagourney, Jim Rutenberg, and Jeff Zeleny, *The New York Times*, November 5, 2008, p. P.1.

"Dueling Brands Pick Up Where Politicians Leave Off," Stuart Elliott, *The New York Times*, November 4, 2008, p. B.3.

"The Politics of Web Strategy," Alwin A.D. Jones, *Black Enterprise*, November 2008, p. 54-55.

"Social Misfits," Caroline Waxler, *Fast Company*, November 2008, p. 160.

"Long by Obama's Side, an Adviser Fills a Role That Exceeds His Title," Jeff Zeleny, *The New York Times*, October 27, 2008, p. A.19.

"Passions: Ryan Black, CEO of Sambazon," Jess McCuan, *Inc.*, October 2008.

"Obama's earnest army; The ground campaign," *The Economist*, October 25, 2008.

"How Innovation Led HTC to the Dream," Kermit Pattison, *Fast Company*, September 2008.

"David Axelrod: Can the 'Axe' cut it…," Tim Shipman, *The Sunday Telegraph*, August 24, 2008, p. 22.

"HASBRO Learns to Spell B-O-T-C-H," Christopher Palmeri and Nandini Lakshman, *BusinessWeek*, August 18, 2008, p. 34.

"The Reader Comment Conundrum," *BusinessWeek* (online), June 12, 2008.

"Smart Leaders: Anne Sellers," Erik Cassano, *Smart Business Indianapolis*, June 2008.

"Getting Engaged: Advertisers Search for Their Voices on YouTube," *Knowledge@Wharton*, April 2, 2008.

"The Pepsi Challenge," Betsy Morris, *Fortune*, February 19, 2008.

"'Motherhood' Returns with Expanded Platform," Shahnaz Mahmud, *Adweek30*, February 10, 2008.

"BW's Businessperson of the Year," *BusinessWeek* (online), Louise Lee, January 3, 2008, p. 1.

"Obama Finds His Address," *The Washington Post*, David Broder, December 23, 2007.

"Social Marketing: How Companies Are Generating Value from Customer Input," *Knowledge@Wharton*, December 2007.

"Star Student Marc Boom," *Modern Healthcare*, September 17, 2007.

"In Praise of Selflessness: Why the Best Leaders Are Servants," Leigh Buchanan, *Inc.*, May 2007.

"Spot the link between a gorilla and chocolate," Alex Benady, *The Independent*, May 14, 2007.

"The Corner Deli That Dared to Break Out of the Neighborhood," Micheline Maynard, *The New York Times*, May 3, 2007, p. C.1.

"Managing a Crisis," *CropLife*, Eric Sfiligoj, April 2007, p. 4.

"In Defense of the Boss from Hell," Jeffrey Pfeffer, *Business 2.0*, March 2007, p. 70.

"Ad-Agency Chief Hammers Out a Sideline as Blacksmith," Patricia Riedman, *Advertising Age*, September 11, 2006, p. 36.

The Audacity of Hope, Barack Obama, Crown Publishing Group, Random House, 2006.

Dreams from My Father, Barack Obama, Crown Publishing Group, Random House, 2004.

"Detroit Free Press Small Business column," *Knight Ridder Tribune Business News*, Carol, January 31, 2005.

It's Your Ship, Mike Abrashoff, Warner Books, Inc., 2002.

"How I Delivered the Goods," Fred Smith, *Fortune*, October 2002.

"Punching out a hoax," Nancy Arnott, *Sales and Marketing Management*, October 1993, p. 12.

"How Obama Manages," Jia Lynn Yang, *Fortune*, July 7, 2008, p.74.

Change.com

CNN.com

Digg.com

LinkedIn.com

My.BarackObama.com

MySpace.com

Nikeplus.com

SecondLife.com

Sribd.com

Twitter.com

Facebook.com

YouTube.com

C

L

M

N

P

R

S